GoodEnoughGov

By

Vincent Watson

ISBN 978-0-578-00934-6

Printed in the USA

Produced by Silentdream Publishing, a subsidiary of Silentdream Enterprises.

Dedication:

I wish to express my sincere thanks to friends who have been supportive in this endeavor and those who provided me with information and answered my questions even though it might have gotten them in trouble at times.

I would also like to thank my family who put up with my moodiness while I worked on this at all hours of the day and night.

Table of Contents:

A few of the major projects going on at DHS and the futility experienced in attempting to execute them.

a. Email Storage & Retention
b. Enterprise Collaboration Portal
c. D2E (Enterprise Email Consolidation)
d. System Monitoring Project
e. SOS Network Integration Project

X: Minnesota Care

This chapter is inconveniently missing, as the people who we willing to talk to me on the side were afraid of abject retaliation should their identities become known. Retaliation as DHS is akin to being cast away on an island full of evil creatures bent on your demise in the most humiliating way possible.

5: Since You Asked… My Conclusions

If it were my government I would…

PREFACE:

In the year since I left DHS, I have traveled a bit, thought about many things and tried to figure out exactly what I wanted to do with myself. My spies at DHS tell me that many things have changed, people have been moved around, left of their own accord, or just generally gotten tired of the bullshit. This is probably a good thing and I know for a fact that a lot of the new oversight was in response to my original website. Even with all of the changes, I understand there is much left to be done and I hope that by publishing this story, more changes will come to pass, and that those at DHS who actually are there to do some good are finally able to do so.

Vincent J. Watson

FORWARD:

In making the decision to write this book, I considered many titles before deciding upon the one the graces the cover of the book you now hold in your hand. Some of those, which were as equally appropriate, include the following.

My Year In Hell
Passive Aggressive Politicking
Your Tax Dollars At Work
And quite a few others…

"My Year in Hell" didn't make the cut because the reality of having chosen to work for "The Man", still grates irritatingly on my psyche, and since the other position in the private sector I was up for at the same time was no longer available. I now know that I have no one to blame but myself for having been so foolishly altruistic in thinking that I could actually make a difference by working for the government of the lovely state I now reside in. (NOTE: I do really like the state I reside in.) I state for the record, and in no unequivocal terms, that what I discovered during my time at DHS is essentially that you really can't make a difference by trying to change a system that embraces failure as it's mandate, regardless of the feelings and priorities of the employees that work there. It was during my first few days at DHS that I was told by someone, whom I do not remember, that DHS doesn't solve problems, but rather spends its time admiring the problem and throwing money at issues until they go away. As you will soon see over the course of this book, the unfortunate truth here is that that statement, although true, is only the tip of the iceberg.

"Passive Aggressive Politicking" didn't make the cut for the simple reason that unless you have worked for a governmental body, you really wouldn't understand the way things are crafted in such passively aggressive manner. To put it more bluntly, as soon as someone smiles at you while agreeing to a particular methodology, you may as well start looking for the knife in your back. It very quickly becomes obvious that a "yes" doesn't necessarily mean that this particular individual sees your point of view, but that they have simply tired of negotiating the particular issue you speak of. It should be noted at this time that readers should keep the phrase "passive aggressive" in mind at all times throughout the reading of this book and that should you happen to work for the State of Minnesota, this particular methodology of working will either be your best friend or your worst enemy, depending on your level of interest in actually getting things done. If you are simply covering your ass until retirement, it works well for reasons that will become apparent in later chapters.

Your Tax Dollars At Work is an obvious misnomer due to the fact that dollars according to DHS management are simply pieces of paper, which may be manipulated into or out of one fund or another for the purpose of justifying a particular individual's position or department's existence. Dollars are manipulated this way for nine months out of the year until a furious volley of activity occurs for the remaining three months in order to hide, spend, or otherwise retain the remaining funds in the budget for projects that were obviously not important enough to be funded and resourced in a timely manner in the first place. Should there not be enough justifiable projects to go around, relatively minor friendships are spawned between individuals or agencies that only months ago would not have pissed on each other if they were on fire. These friendships tend to last about as long as your average trip to the bathroom, and are as quickly flushed once a secure location for the remaining funds has been creatively conjured out of someone's ass. Then at the end of year, when budget sweeps are over, those friendships are dissolved, and the game starts all over again.

> *The official line on the Minnesota Department of Human Services is that The Minnesota Department of Human Services touches the lives of one in four Minnesotans with a variety of services intended to help people live as independently as possible. DHS is the state's largest agency, with an annual budget of nearly $9 billion and approximately 7,200 employees located throughout Minnesota. The Minnesota Department of Human Services helps people meet their basic needs by providing or administering health care coverage, economic assistance, and a variety of services for children, people with disabilities and older Minnesotans.*

I find this statement to be absolutely true, and horribly frightening at the same time. In the course of writing this book, I have walked into many public places and been able to solicit many absolute horror stories from people whom I have never met and have had dealings with DHS, and very few of them were positive.

I will say that in the end that the concept of human services is a noble one, but that it assumes that the structure of the agency is one which promotes providing those services to people who's paycheck isn't signed by the current administration and who actually need those services in a timely manner. This will never happen for reasons that will be explained during the course of this book.

For myself, the title "GoodEnoughGov" seemed the most appropriate because it is a term that most of us have either heard or used for most of our lives to explain the base inadequacies of our governmental bodies. It is also a term that fulfills our need to explain away the political facts, rumors and speculations that have, for the most part, become part of our daily lives in our quest to get ahead or simply survive the controls mandated by the incompetent dimwits we were dumb enough to elect in the first place.

Having used this term for most of my life, and usually in a conversation with someone else who has also used the term, I can state for the record that without a doubt unless you work there, you really have no fucking idea how deep the bullshit and bureaucracy run in those hallowed halls of government.

I do promise that by the time you complete this book, you will begin to understand the dysfunctional way this segment of your government is run and why your hard-earned dollars are pissed away into several State run black holes, of which I will focus on the State of Minnesota Department of Human Services in particular.

By reading this book you will understand the following:

> *How many millions of your tax dollars are pissed away on bad projects and even worse management of those projects.*
>
> *How the state hires contractors (some of whom are not even US citizens) to manage state employees, and how those contractors are allowed to manage budgets and projects to their own benefit when a US citizen could do the job just as well and for a lot less money.*

How the state hires contractors for years at a time and at salaries far above that of state employees in order to keep extra positions open and not lose the funding allocated for that extra position.

How and why I was asked to falsify documents and change numbers on reports requested by other agencies to cover up the incompetent management mistakes made in DHS and to secure the position of particular individuals and agencies.

Why the governor's ***"Drive To Excellence"*** *program will fail because the agencies refuse to cooperate with each other.*

How vendors are chosen to the benefit of a particular individual instead of negotiating the best deal for the state.

Why, when I brought up the possibility of state employees and contractors being "on the take", I was immediately pulled off projects to keep me from investigating further.

How critical infrastructure information is manipulated or withheld from other agencies to keep them reliant on DHS.

How, when I suggested that the state was paying exorbitant prices for computer equipment and software, my Director was told it was inappropriate for me to question already negotiated state purchasing contracts.

How personality conflicts, instead of the need of the general public, often dictate departmental policies and methodologies.

How millions of dollars in state owned computer equipment is not tracked and occasionally simply disappears, and why no one seems to care.

How employees manipulate scheduling and benefits using well-known loopholes in the system and thus end up providing substandard services and response times in emergency situations.

How the union protects employees, so that employees can keep their jobs despite blatant rule violations or illegal activities.

How vendor contracts are decided upon and manipulated to benefit of individuals and departments, even though it may not be the best deal for the state.

How MinnesotaCare spends millions of dollars on unnecessary projects while at the same time denying benefits to those most in need of their services.

Why projects take months or years instead of days or weeks.

Why people with no practical experience in their area are allowed to manage projects into failure, and how the money for these projects is bounced around from agency to agency to avoid having it reallocated.

How and why official data requests are buried or manipulated even though the state mandates the free and open exchange of non-private information when requested.

How the project initiation (charter) works and why it is likely that a very much needed public project will never get funded.

And much, much more...

It is said that if you are not angry, then you are not paying attention. Hopefully this book will make you pay attention and maybe, get a little angry.

Hopefully it will make you at least angry enough to write your legislators, and representatives to tell them that enough is enough.

If enough of you write to them and tell them how angry you are, maybe they will at least begin to try and fix the system, which is why we hired them in the first place.

If they do that, then maybe we will get better roads, services, and all of the other things they promised us when they asked us to vote them into office.

And maybe, just maybe, a few more single parents will get approved for healthcare because we didn't piss away millions of dollars of useless projects.

And yes I know that some of those "dimwits" are appointed "dimwits" and not elected. But to give you an idea of how that process works, consider the following.

The State has very specific rules against nepotism and yet, year after year, children, friends, relatives of friends, and just plain friends continue to show up as employees during periods of random availability such as school breaks.

I wouldn't be so damned frustrated by this practice if these people actually did some work. But hiring your daughter (who happens to be home from school for the summer) to sit around in case someone might need some copying done seems a bit off the mark.

Now, those things said, I wish to apologize to those wonderful people who work for the Department of Human Services and all of the other state agencies and go the extra mile to do their jobs well and attempt to make a difference. There are many of them, and unfortunately most of them are not mentioned here due to the enormous amount of space the dimwits take up.

The desire and ability to do one's job in an expeditious and skillful manner, despite having to wade through pools of bureaucracy and bullshit, take a special kind of person.

I'm talking the climbing to the top of Mount Everest "because it's there" kind of special person. I'm talking the person who shows up and fights for that last inch of progress not only because a thing need to be done, but because it is the right thing to do.

I'm talking that kind of commitment that keeps one locked up in a South African Prison for the better part of your life when a simple denouncement of previously stated ideologies would have you sipping piña coladas by the poolside the very next afternoon. Thanks Nelson.

I'm talking the kind of people who do the right thing, for the right reason even if the end result is only partial success. These are the people for whom I am writing this book.

These are the people who deserve to have state provided waders handed out before each meeting and for whom the elected dimwits should be forced to clean them afterwards.

It is those people I salute, and hopefully if nothing else, the end result of this book will be that someone who is elected pays attention, provides some oversight, and worries less about the next election and more about the reasons they were put into office in the first place.

One more thing…

I would be hard pressed to keep all of the names and faces straight unless I come up with some sort of matrix designed to keep all of the players coordinated for you my dear reader. The Lawyers tell me that since all state information, employees, salaries, etc is considered public information, I do not even need go through the trouble of changing all of the names to protect the innocent – so to speak.

This is rather a good thing, as there really aren't any innocents here and everyone mentioned in this book exists in one form or another, and quite likely in the exact form in which they are described here.

While a few things may have changed since the actual writing of this book and its subsequent publishing, you may assume quite correctly that the people here do exist and may even be friends or acquaintances of yours.

By the time the book is actually published, I am pretty sure that those responsible for such obvious mismanagement will have attempted some sort of disguise and tried to hide or cover up at least some of the insanity. I am not that worried about it. The bullshit is so deep at the Minnesota Department of Human Services that it would take several years and a complete housecleaning to remove even a tiny bit of the smell that resides there.

However, in an attempt to keep the players straight, I will identify the players in this drama by their initials and add a numeric value in the event of duplication of initials.

Contractors noted similarly and identified as such. State contractors are a unique case and in most cases uniquely despised for their ability to skirt the system while being paid exorbitant sums of money over a long period of time for a number of reasons. Remember I said this when you are introduced to **GO**.

Departmental entities or agencies will be identified as they were structured at the time or referred to by their abbreviated title. For example, The State of Minnesota Office of Enterprise Technology will be referred to as OET.

Projects or Initiatives will similarly be referred to as they were structured. For example the Information Technology Zones of Control Initiative will be referred to as ZOCA.

I will also, for the sake of expeditious processes, concede here and now that the events described here are from my memory and are as accurate as I could make them given the fact that I no longer have access to most of these people or these particular circumstances. Knowing how the data request process is manipulated, I am also sure that I will not be able to gain access to documents I request.

The excellent thing about government is that there are always people there who are frustrated by the waste and incompetent management that are more than willing to provide insider information provided their identities remain confidential.

Documentation will be provided as required and available, and copies of these documents can be found at the website promoting this book. I have this documentation because even though I may have been a state employee, I am also a taxpayer and it is my perfect right to march my disgruntled ass into the main lobby of any particular government agency and demand any document that does not fall into the category of protected information. There are those, particularly the evil spawn of CZ, who will swear that I am just pissed off because I was terminated. He is only marginally correct. Yes, I am pissed off about having wasted a year of my life in futility, but the rest of it firmly stems around the fact that it is the system itself that is screwed up and were I to be given the option of working for another government agency or being poked in the eye with a sharp stick, I would first need to see the stick.

> *IDEA #1: If you suspect your state employed spouse is cheating on you and communicating with his or her lover while at work, or that your state employed neighbor is embezzling your hard earned tax dollars to fund fishing expeditions to Alaska, you are perfectly entitled to stroll your ass on down there and demand every email, phone log, post-it note, toilet paper sheet, or any other communication that you think you require to*

prove your case, and they have to give it to you. OK, it's not exactly that easy, but pretty close to that easy.

IDEA #2: Every person on the planet with a disability should stroll down the closest government office with a job opening and apply for pretty much everything. They are so paranoid about discrimination lawsuits that you are almost guaranteed to be hired. This is not to say that you should apply for things for which you are not qualified, or have no interest in, but it's simply to say that it's harder for them to hide behind rules and regulations and / or, their own biases.

You may also assume that eventually there will be one or more of them who will bitch, piss and moan about how they were represented unfairly and call me a liar and complain that I am not telling the truth about them, and I'm ok with that because those people most likely fall into the retirement slug category and couldn't be trusted to wipe their own ass without getting some on their hand. If they were doing the job they were hired to do sufficiently, they probably wouldn't be mentioned here in the first place. To those people, I issue the following promise: "I'll take a polygraph if you will."

On a final note, I fully believe that most people who work for the state of Minnesota DHS are good people with good intentions and a strong desire to thrive in a sea of sharks that determined to devour them.

The problem is with the system. The system rewards incompetence while ignoring the abuse that comes with a job that no one is afraid of losing. My suggestion is that all state jobs be just as renewable as those of elected officials. If all state jobs were renewable, there would be incentive for people to accomplish the tasks set before them. They would be creative, productive and motivated to provide services to those in need by doing the jobs they were hired to do.

Ask anyone seeking a state job why they wish to work for the state and they will give you one word, "security". The thing is that once you are in, you are in.

Well that may be true, but it's not exactly the best way to run a company, or a state, or any governmental entity.

This is why the constitution was written the way it was written. It tried to ensure that "we the people" got a say in the operation of our government and to have the ability to eject those simply consuming resources and providing nothing in return.

It was written that way to ensure that we could correct the mistakes we would inevitably make, and that is why we have periodic elections – so we can recycle the dimwits once in a while. Unfortunately, the dimwits got there first and managed to twist, distort, and manipulate the original wishes of the founding fathers.

This is unfortunate because it's not really that difficult to do the job you were hired to do and provide the services you were hired to provide given any decent amount of skill and motivation. Nuff said.

CHAPTER 1
INTRODUCTIONS:

The cast of characters at DHS is numerous, and therefore I will be concentrating only on those that I have had direct contact with and who play a significant part in the projects I am attempting to describe. The minor characters will be identified by their initials, as previously stated. However, additional information may not be provided where it would serve no specific purpose or would serve to embarrass someone or subject them to retaliation by DHS management. You do remember what I said about retaliation, don't you?

Appropriate documentation will be provided, or reprinted at the end of this book, to enhance your experience – or simply to explain statements that may be not as easily understood by someone not in the DHS inner circle. Copies of documents and diagrams that provide additional information will either be presented here or on the website for clarity. Emails will be printed in their entirety so that you may understand the complete chain of events leading up to the situation at hand.

Speculative statements, rumors, or other possibly non-factual statements will be noted as such and you may consider this the official statement of disclaimer. Office rumors, of course, are to be taken with the grain of salt that they usually represent. However, they are stated here in cases where a particular rumor may serve to emphasize a particular individual's level of credibility, as well as the credibility of those charged with dealing with said individual.

Quotes from specific individuals will be noted as such and where disputes may arise, I again will be happy to take a polygraph as long as the individual presenting the dispute agrees to do so as well, and at their own expense.

These things said, let's start from the top.

The Department of Human Services encompasses most of the state-sponsored agencies charged with providing services to the general public and those of a non-specific, public-interest nature. That is to say, mostly medical and legal services, but also other peripheral services such as "child support, aging services, economic assistance, chemical and mental health services, etc.

As I have previously stated, these are all excellent and required services, but the department itself, having succumbed to inept policies and management, is only able to provide these services on a limited basis. Those of you who have attempted to utilize these services will immediately identify with the frustration of attempting to obtain one of these services when needed and the endless futility that results in this process.

The short answer is that you will most likely never be able to get what you need when you need it, and if and when you finally do, its probably too late as you are already living in some relative's basement listening through the vents in the middle of the night about how "inconvenient" it is to have you there.

But here I digress, as I am not really here to debate the politics of how they run DHS, but to tell the story of how it could actually get around to the actual business of providing services and save a few million bucks at the same time. The fact that you will learn about how they do things at DHS is merely an added bonus, and oddly enough, these millions of dollars could be used to provide those much-needed services. Those things said, let's move on to the introductions.

YOUR HUMBLE NARRATOR: VW – (DHS - ARCH & ENG MANAGER)

I joined DHS on December 13th of 2006 as the Architectural & Engineering Manager for Information Technology Services after interviewing with the DHS ITS director, CZ and a contractor from Canada GO. Oddly enough, I never actually ended up managing the Architects in this enterprise for reasons that will become apparent later in this tale. I came to DHS from the private sector, having spent the previous fifteen or so years in various management roles in information technology. The private sector is still very political as you know, but in the long run, they are also very, very much motivated by their ability to make money by providing products and services to their particular industry.

The politics in the private sector seem to be, in my experience, limited to pissing contests between personalities – as opposed to immediate self-preservation. For the most part, you work hard, you produce, you make money, and you survive. Do not accomplish these things, and someone from HR shows up at your desk with an empty copy paper box and your final check asking you to follow the guy in uniform out the front door.

Government work has no such credo. Ask anyone who works in the public sector what they enjoy about their job; the answer is usually the same: "It's secure". Let's face it, rumor has it that there is a special place in hell reserved for public servants and having been one of those public servants for almost a year, I feel fully vindicated in saying that that special place simply cannot be any worse than the actual public service.

What they actually do is "admire the problem" as opposed to actually solving it. You, my humble reader and member of the tax paying public, really have no idea how much money is "thrown" at a problem because of inept management and how much time is wasted in meetings and political wrangling when the truth of the matter is that a one hour meeting and a big stick held by the right person could solve the problem in no time at all.

While I have no disillusionments with regard to job security, I cringe at the actual differences, which roughly translated amount to: "It's practically impossible for me to get fired no matter how much of a slug I am when working for the public sector." This is very true. As far as I can tell, there are two things which will get your sorry ass immediately walked out of the door: surfing for porn on the Internet, and killing someone in the lobby during business hours in front of a video camera.

Everything else requires all sorts of political wrestling matches, a complicated series of investigations, the filing of union grievances, and much personal time and aggravation, during which you are relegated to a corner with full pay and the stigma of having the boys from security show up at your desk to replace your hard drive while they take the old one to a dark room to plow through the bits and bytes looking for evidence that your misdeeds are somehow documented on your hard drive.

If you are a minority, you have an extra ace in the hole because they simply do not want to be put in the situation of having someone accuse them of racial discrimination. I admit that those who happen to be minority, but just as useless as their Caucasian counterparts, all too often use this, but the truth of the matter is that if you are indeed useless and happen to be minority, it works.

So why did I take the job you ask? Simply put, I took the job because it was secure. Since moving to Minnesota in 1991, I have worked for five companies;

two of them went bankrupt, and one of them spent two years in bankruptcy and then moved their IT headquarters to Cleveland, (yes, there was no way in hell I was moving to Cleveland). In fact, I think Cleveland is where that special place in hell for public servants is located.

The fourth was a school that expected me to teach the ins and outs of networking without any actual networking equipment and then seemed surprised when I suddenly refused to keep lugging my own personal equipment in from home.

So yes, I fell for the bullshit lines about security and benefits. I mean, what the hell; I have a family to feed, so you may call me a hypocrite if you wish, but read on for the whole story. At the end of September of 2006, I received an eight page job description and the invitation to interview for this position. I figured, what the hell, at least the State of Minnesota more than likely would not be moving to Cleveland anytime soon. The Job Description is reprinted at the end of this book. Never mind that I never got to do any of the things on it.

To give you an idea of how long things take to get done, I interviewed for this position in October, was told in November that I was the number one choice, and then was unable to start until December 13th. I mean WTF. Either you need someone or you do not, and meanwhile I was balancing other interviews and one confirmed job offer around, thinking that whatever happened I was secure in obtaining a position. Rumor has it that dealing with DHS HR is an incredibly complex process where your chances of being hit by lightening before the position you are attempting to hire for is filled is greater than actually filling the position.

During this process, I also called my father who had worked for the city of Chicago for 40 years who asked me over and over again; "are you sure you want to work for government?" Of course my answer was, "probably not, but what the hell, how bad could it really be?" This was the question I asked my self right up to the day I was to start my career at DHS, and unfortunately I was about to find out.

While I am sure that he knew something I didn't, he wasn't one to cover the sweet smell of excellent benefits in a cloud of disillusionment and I could tell by the hesitancy in his voice that this was going to be no picnic. In hindsight, I wish that he had waved me off this disaster, as it would have saved me a ton of aggravation and I would have spent the last year in corporate America, collecting stock options, a lot more money, and far fewer headaches.

I worked for DHS for exactly three hundred and sixty one days when, citing philosophical differences, my director decided not to confirm my position with the state – one-week before my probation was up. Essentially, she meant that she took objection to me questioning all of the crap that was going on there, my refusing to fire two employees with whom I had had absolutely no experience, and not adequately covering up her incompetent management mistakes. Despite my decision on the name of this book, it truly was a year in hell, but let's jump into the introductions.

CZ – (DHS / IT DIRECTOR)

CZ was my Director and apparently in charge of the ITS department for the State of Minnesota Department of Human Services Central Office and all of its peripheral components.

The central office component of the Department of Human Services Information Systems Technology division is divided into five distinct components with each being led by a manager or supervisor. These components are detailed in the following paragraphs. CZ is a late 50ish, grandma type who likes to tell stories about her life during meetings – as opposed to actually getting things done when scheduled to talk about DHS projects.

Instead of talking about the DHS issues we were scheduled to talk about, we all learned about her grandchildren, her home and how much she paid for it, the dock she seems to be unable to get out of the lake behind her home, the tree in her back yard which she suspects her previous neighbor of killing to improve the view of the previously mentioned lake, the reasons why her ex-husband no longer gardens, and any other this or that which she deems appropriate conversation instead of the actual meeting you are supposed to be having to discuss work.

I can honestly say that I know more about her personal life than I do about agency projects, priorities, and agency staffing. Almost any meeting you might have with CZ could very easily be accomplished in 15 minutes or less, but usually takes several hours in order to wade through the trivialities of her life. God, I wanted to reach across the table and strangle her almost every time we met.

In case you were wondering, according to CZ, the reason her ex-husband no longer gardens is because he told her "every time he digs a hole, he imagines her in it." Think what you will, but since that story came straight from her mouth, I take it as gospel – as she has repeated it to myself no less than five times and to others just as many. If she spent as much time working on DHS projects as she did bullshitting about her life, her "very full schedule", as she puts it, would usually be empty. Those of you who have attended these meetings already know what a joke they are, but for those of you who have not, you need to understand that I am not exaggerating in the slightest. Conversations that could be and should be handled in five minutes or less, can take hours.

CZ lords over her minions with all the grace and style of Benito Mussolini. That is to say that she rules through fear and intimidation – most likely due to her lack of knowledge of the facts she pretends to be an authority on in order to keep her job. This combined with her desire to cover up bad management, departmental errors and other non-trivial errors in judgment causes her sense of paranoia to skyrocket.

Never one to let those pesky facts, or even reality, get in the way of her cushy state pension, actual knowledge of the facts or intelligence is rarely a factor in dealing with her and her reality is often distorted by her to represent her own personal demented concepts of what she is there to accomplish. No wonder they hung Benito's hairy ass from that lamppost in the streets of Italy.

I do realize that friendships are a part of the daily office environment and that people do need to develop personal relationships at work. Yes, people usually do this by discussing their lives outside of the office, but there has to be a limit to this and she is completely unaware of those limits.

The funny thing is, everyone knows these things about her, and yet there she is miss-managing millions of state dollars. Absolutely no one likes or respects this woman, and rumor has it that her manager has warned her in the past for her aggressive and threatening management style. So we have to ask ourselves, why then is she still there?

CZ never does any actual work, but delegates the work to her direct reports. Those in this precarious position know that Chris is not so much concerned with the facts as she is with saving face and garnering favors with her peers. NEVER, EVER bring her numbers that contradict something she has said (even if the numbers she said were so fucking wrong that the ground shifted when she uttered them) or something she indicated to her manager without her having known all of the facts, which she does quite often. Doing this will immediately result in several sessions of mad rants and raves followed by instructions on how the numbers should actually look and a staunch dressing down on how incompetent you are when it was her fucking error in the first place.

When asked for reports, ninety percent of the numbers I presented were re-manipulated by her prior to being distributed to the requesting agency without any regard for their accuracy, but rather to match her desires for the organization. As I said before, CZ is never one to let the facts get in the way of her opinion of what should be.

The other thing that I find amusing is that apparently she came to the State of Minnesota quite a while ago, from a rather large Minneapolis based financial institution where she was an accountant or something. The more observant of you will realize the following; (THIS MEANS SHE HAS NO TECHNICAL BACKGROUND) and of course this will all become very apparent very soon in our story.

GO – (DHS / CONTRACTOR/PROJECT MANAGER/NOT A US CITIZEN)

GO is a contractor hired by CZ as a project manager when DHS built their new building in downtown St. Paul. GO is a smart guy who is marginally interesting with decent technical knowledge. GO lives in Toronto and commutes to Minnesota for two or three days per week to manage all of the large IT projects for CZ. He also has the people skills of a mentally challenged Siberian Yak, and yet makes an ass load of money, which is paid for by your tax dollars.

Did you want to go back and read that again? I'll wait.

OK, I have no issues with contractors, or Canadians per se, but contractors are a dime a dozen in the Twin Cities and you can't swing a dead cat in Minnesota without knocking over a computer contractor or technical project manager. CZ has also tasked GO with negotiating vendor contracts and the final say in the selection of vendors in spite of the fact that contractors are not allowed to manage state employees or negotiate contracts for reasons which will become quite obvious.

Yes, this sort of arrangement is technically against the law, but since there is no real oversight, no one seems to notice. The rumor, and my firm belief, is that he is completely on the take (also against the law), which is the reason he stays around subjecting himself to her irrational management style. I asked her about this once, and it seemed like it was all she could do not to reach across the table and smack the cocoa beige off my face.

If he isn't on the take, I would appreciate having it explained to me how he is allowed to bypass agency staffing, and consistently hire the same vendors time after time even to install products that all of the ITS staff believes are the wrong products. The first rule of business is that if you are not the most competent person in a particular position, you surround yourself with people who are.

CZ has done the opposite. She has surrounded herself with people whom she can manipulate and control, and she has installed contractors in place of managers to manage her subordinates because these particular contractors have it way too good to rock the boat, and bide their time while laughing all the way to the bank.

I would also appreciate it if would someone please tell me how is it possible that CZ managed to convince the state of Minnesota that the only good contractor in North America lives in another country, and should be paid to commute to work in the office two or three days a week? GO pretends that he pays for his own travel, however it would seem to anyone of average intelligence that he is making well enough to cover those expenses and his time in the air.

This also means that CZ had to fill out the paperwork; she had to get him a US work visa; and she had to get the funding to fly this guy from there to here and back every week, in addition to his contractor level salary. How is that appropriate in any way whatsoever?

This isn't fucking NAFTA. This is a guy who holds an occasional meeting which is usually over the phone, subverts resources from other departments on a whim and with CZ's blessing, chooses products and solutions that the rest of the ITS staff does not agree with and then hires his own vendors to do the work. Any idiot, preferably an American idiot, could do that and you my humble reader are paying for it.

I don't know about you, but that kind of pisses me off. If I were you, I would download the data request form from the state website, request copies of the

DHS ITS contract for this idiot and send it in to your state representative asking for a refund.

By the way, I need to take this moment to apologize to Siberian Yaks everywhere, but you were the first thing to come to mind.

BG – (DHS / OPERATIONS MANAGER)

BG is another interesting character, but is definitely a card-carrying member of the "talksalot" contingent. If you ask BG a question, you had better really want the answer, in fact several answers. If you have a conversation near her, expect her to join in – often changing the topic entirely so that she can join in. She loves to make it about "HER".

To be perfectly honest, I actually admire BG for her unswerving ability to shovel horseshit with the best of them, as she is definitely a survivor. A random technical term here or there, and the ability to keep it all straight in one's head, is an admirable trait but makes for a lousy manager. You can also be assured that anything you say to BG will go straight back to CZ, so you had better watch your ass in this regard. This is another interesting issue, as BG spent the first week I was at DHS telling me about all of the people I could and could not trust and it turned out that she is one of the ones that I couldn't.

I state for clarity that I do not believe BG to be malicious or un-intelligent, but that BG has been with DHS for so long, she is no longer capable of independent thought. BG is the person in one of those alien movies that is consumed by the alien but not digested, and has in fact become part of the monster.

Those things said, she knows the agency well, and maintains the attention to detail in dealing with issues we all should be proud of, and has figured out how to manage the tangles of episodic paranoia that CZ requires for herself and from her managers. I do realize that this is more self-preservation than actual knowledge, but more people would be willing to tolerate it if she would just shut the fuck up once in a while and listen to what someone else had to say instead of constantly yak, yak, yakking.

JH – (DHS / DESKTOP SUPERVISOR)

JH is a good guy and maintains a level of artistic stoicism that would be admired by Zeno himself. To watch JH in a meeting where the bullshit is flying far and high is truly impressive and would serve well as a performance art piece in a window exhibit in a downtown department store.

JH keeps to himself, follows the rules to the letter, and most importantly practices what he preaches – which means that he is one of the good ones. JH realizes that there is no easy way out of the circumstances currently at DHS and thus had decided to follow the rules without variation or betraying his obvious contempt for the system. I would define JH as someone lives to do things well despite the obvious aversion to actual project completion that breeds throughout DHS. I do worry about him sometimes as it is always the quiet ones that end up snapping –where you get to see the neighbor on CNN tell everyone what a nice quiet boy he was. Although I do not expect JH to "Snap," I am sure that the little voice that resides in all of our heads is present in his, and the same people on his list are the very same ones on everyone else's.

I did play what I hope was a rather nasty trick on JH when I left by "nuking" the hard drive on my laptop so that no data could ever be recovered. I am pretty sure that CZ's paranoia would have kicked in and she most likely would have asked him to see what was on the laptop when it was returned.

There was nothing bad on the laptop, as I rarely used it and then only for work, however, I am sure they will spend about a week trying to recover something that isn't there and I pretty sure that with CZ being the paranoid individual she is, the fact that I even bothered her will drive her absolutely bat shit. Sorry JH, it really wasn't about you at all.

LM – (DHS / Application Development Supervisor)

LM is relatively new at DHS having joined the agency in the summer of 2007. I get the feeling that LM is slightly over her head and has yet to figure out the balance of managing processes and making everyone happy – that is to say that she wants to make everyone happy. This is too bad because I actually like LM, and it is unfortunate that she will more than likely be one of those that concedes the match and becomes one of the drones. Please do not misconstrue my earlier statement to mean that we should not strive to make everyone happy. We are here to provide the aforementioned services in the best way we can, and it is quite refreshing to meet someone willing to at least attempt this feat.

NT – (DHS / APPLICATIONS ARCHITECH)

NT is another interesting character. My first impression of her was that she was evil wicked, mean, and nasty. My second impression of her was that she was evil wicked, mean, and nasty. However, having gotten to know her, you soon realize that her bulldog like determination is a great asset and tends to provide for her ability to pound square pegs into round holes while fighting off those trying to kick her in the teeth at the same time.

This is to say that she has been around long enough to learn the system well, and uses this knowledge to navigate the shark-infested waters that is DHS better than anyone else I have seen.

If you want a person hired and the complicated process of dealing with HR managed you call NT because, as I have said before, dealing with the HR department is for lack of a better term, "a mutherfucker".

If you would like a project moved forward in accordance with established policies and procedures, when everyone else wants something else completely off the mark, you send NT. NT's methodology works well and serves DHS well, however disconcerting it may be at first to get to know and have to deal with her. She also always has candy on her table full of all of the things you forgot you liked as a kid, which is a good thing.

It would be nice if she could accomplish this without bulldozing through the universe like a sun about to go supernova, but apparently she had learned the system well and decided to deal with the fact that if you want something done at DHS, you don't take any shit from anyone.

JB – (DHS / CIO)

JB is the CIO for DHS. It was at least 3 months after I started at DHS before Johanna spoke to me or even acknowledged my existence. This is more due to the culture of the DHS silo system, and the Top Down hierarchy than due to any unfortunate snobbery on her part. People at DHS normally do not talk to people more than one or two rungs down the ladder from them. I am not sure what the reasoning is for this, but in attending many meetings with the upper management types on the eighth floor, you soon learn that anyone above you knows without question that they are above you and immediately go out of their way to make sure that you know it as well.

If you will remember my earlier statement regarding the distinct departmentalization of the agency, for the most part, you speak to those with whom you require direct contact to and no one else. CZ will also make damned sure that your contact with upper-management is extremely limited, which I attribute to her obvious paranoia.

JB however is a different case. JB, despite her cold exterior, maintains an absolute sense of professionalism and simply gets down to the business at hand. I worked on several projects with JB, and the great thing about her is that when you leave a meeting with her, you know what needs to be done, who needs to do it, and when it needs to be done. This is in direct contrast to CZ's meetings where everyone walks away asking, "what the fuck just happened and why does my ass hurt?"

The things I haven't figured out are her ulterior motives. CZ goes out of her way to make it seems as if JB is an insane tyrant and bully, who is constantly on the prowl for someone's ass to rip into for having embarrassed the department. I later learned that ninety-nine percent of this was CZ's own paranoia more than anything else. It was either that or that JB actually is a psychotic dictator with the ability to hide it well. At this point, nothing would surprise me.

While I have no doubt that if you cross JB, she will be more than happy to rip you a new one, I have yet to see it happen. Maybe she delegates this all out to her minions, e.g. "CZ", but I have a feeling that CZ's paranoia in this regard stems from the fact that she needs to have her medicinal dosage upped.

For the record, I am not stating here any actual knowledge of her requiring any sort of mental medication. I am merely pointing out that having known many people over the years that behaved with similarly high levels of paranoia and anxiety, who happened to be cured by heavy doses of a psychotropic medication such a Prozac, or say lithium, that I find the similarities between her behavior and those that I have known who were not treated in any way whatsoever quite interesting.

SL – (DHS / BUSINESS RELATIONS TEAM)

SL is an interesting case in that she doesn't really work for ITS. SL is one of those people who puts her money where her mouth is and isn't shy about it. SL used to work for Healthcare, but made the mistake of disagreeing with her boss at a meeting in front of her other coworkers. SL was then what we call in government work "marginalized".

As I have stated before, it's a bitch to fire someone once they have passed their probationary period. To this end, if someone in power decides that you have become more of a liability, or in this case simply doesn't like you, you get put into a corner, with nothing to do. The scary part about all of this is that this goes on all the time. There are at least five or six people in DHS, that I know of, who have been had this happen to them.

Having been marginalized, you receive no tasks, no projects, no… nothing. You collect your pay and spend eight hours a day surfing the web, scratching your ass, and picking your nose, whatever. The goal is of course to bore the living shit out of you until you quit of your own accord, or they wait until you click on some innocuous link on a web page that diverts to a porn site and then they accuse you of downloading porn – at which point they can get rid of you.

The problem with this theory is that people usually don't quit. There is no way in hell that you are going to get someone who has spent the last twenty years building up a pension to simply walk out of the door unless they are an absolute idiot, so they simply sit and wait out retirement or the state waits until they fuck up by surfing to the wrong site, coming back fifteen seconds late from lunch, etc.

The only other way around this is to cut one of those afore mentioned deals with another area and send the offending individual away with the money that they would normally cost you. SL had been marginalized for about a year before CZ made a deal with her previous boss to transfer her to ITS.

SL came to ITS still marginalized on a trade between CZ and one of her old friends in Healthcare until someone finally realized that she would make a great project manager. SL manages the communications between ITS and its customers, which is unfortunate because that means that she spends a lot of time telling the customer that ITS is so fucked up that their project will either never be completed or is several months behind schedule.

SL is definitely one of the Mount Everest People.

AH – (DHS / BUSINESS RELATIONS TEAM / CONTRACTOR)

AH is a contractor that was originally hired to work on architectural projects, but has since been moved to the BRT "Business Relationship Team" to also handle communications and project charters. AH is a relatively good guy who also happens to know which side of the fence is greener. That is to say that if you are not part of the solution, there is excellent money to be made in prolonging the problem.

Working with AH is like working building a tower with triangular bricks instead of rectangular ones. He wants to use the triangular ones because it takes longer and will more than likely require extensive and constant reworking – which means that he gets to keep his cushy job.

A conversation about a new project with AH usually goes like this:

You: I want to build a website.

AH: What color do you want it?

You: Doesn't matter.

AH: Well, I'll schedule a meeting with 15 uninvolved people to decide about the color before we proceed.

You: But I don't care about the color.

AH: You can't build a website without the color being known first.

You: The color is out of the scope of this project.

AH: Fine, I'll schedule the meeting to decide the color.

Are you listening DHS internal customers? And you still were wondering why your project would never get done?

MS – (PMO / PROJECT MANAGER)

MS is a project manager from the Projects Management Office of ITS. From my experience, she has zero technical background; she also has zero project management experience or training. I guess this is why she is often asked to manage ITS technical projects, and why they never, ever get completed. I have worked with MS on several projects, and I cannot imagine a more frustrating, futile, idiotic decision making process to save my life.

You have all heard the keep it simple stupid quote. This quote is designed around the fact that some things are simple, will always be simple, and do not require any sort of complexity whatsoever. If you want to drag a project on, and on, until absolute failure is achieved, get MS involved and you won't be disappointed.

Given this obvious lack of experience in the area for which she has been tasked to manage projects, I find it highly amusing that she is even remotely involved with managing ITS projects. Working with MS is akin to asking me to do brain surgery. I am not trained in it, and tugging on the wrong thing is highly inadvisable, but MS would slice your head open and start poking around leaving an absolute mess, and then blame the designers for lack of the documentation she never requested in the first place.

One interesting thing about her is that her husband manages all of the purchasing for DHS ITS, which means that if you piss her off, your purchasing decisions have the ability to become very interesting.

EC – (DHS / ENGINEERING SUPERVISOR)

EC was one of my direct reports, having been with DHS since the entirety of the ITS department computer farm consisted of a palm pilot and a soup can telephone system.

EC, in some ways, is a remarkable guy but suffers from the belief that dissemination of information leads to loss of control. The amount of technical knowledge kept in his head is actually quite remarkable, however his ability to manage others based on this information is constantly in question because of the random storage and retrieval system that tends to fail in most humans. The problem with this is that it makes managing this information impossible, as having such massive amounts of information in your head with no discernable way of organizing it makes it difficult to manage projects.

Because DHS has grown so quickly with the advancement of technology and the high level of paranoia CZ mandates in her reports, it is difficult for him to accomplish tasks in any organized manner and therefore everything is done in very small bits and pieces over very long periods of time.

The difficulties in managing an IT department based on a consistently confusing state of mismanagement will become quite apparent later in our tale, but it should be sufficient to say at this point that EC would have made a good supervisor had his previous managers been more interested in level of accomplishment instead of absolute domination and guardianship of the department. More on EC will be forthcoming.

SB – (DHS / ENGINEER LEVEL 4)

SB was a level four system engineer who worked for ITS during the first 8 months of my arrival. I say worked because SB left us for another position due to the fact that she was no longer able to be effective as an engineer at DHS.

I won't get into the details at this time, but you will soon see what I mean, and those of you who know or knew SB will relish the tale of who she actually was and what she was really about.

I think we all know someone who probably got the raw end of a deal at the office, and while I won’t go that far at this point, I only mention it because it will inevitably prove to show that almost any problem can usually be solved, assuming that those involved are actually willing to work to solve the problem at hand and in the case of SB, this simply wasn’t the case on either side. For the moment I will attribute this to the fact that at some point she simply gave up, and for the record, I don’t fucking blame her.

NB – (DHS / ENTERPRISE SYSTEMS ARCHITECT)

NB is the DHS Enterprise Systems Architect. If you have ever seen one of the “Grumpy Old Men” movies, you have an excellent idea of who NB is or rather what he is like.

I like NB, as he is old school IT that most likely evolved through the ranks of information technology throughout the years, but he has aged past the realm of being able to “keep up with the Jones’s”.

NB’s view of statewide information technology architecture is for the most part right on the money. However, what surprises me is that in his twenty plus years of working at state positions in IT, he seems to understand the system well, but not the nuances of implementation through adversity. I will give him this particular notion, as at some point you simply just have to stop believing in the system. The effective result of this is that CZ gives him relative autonomy in pretty much everything so all he needs to do is show up for the occasional meeting and either agree or disagree and then disappear. I guess it's good work if you can get it.

Even I, with my limited time there, managed to figured out that rumblings of frustration not only serve to cause your opponents to dig their feet in, but also to expose your back directly to the knife. In other words, when presented with surgery, we tend to not want the straight "A" doctor, but rather prefer the "B" doctor who has successfully completed the procedure you are undergoing hundreds of times.

Although CZ respects his opinion on technology decisions and thinks very well of NB, she might find it interesting to find out that the reverse is not true. In what are usually very entertaining conversations with NB, the word stupid, immediately followed by BINT, is quite often involved. Even he knows what a technologically incompetent tyrant she is.

I know that I have said this before, but what keeps popping into my head is that I find it so interesting that everyone at the state realizes that this woman should not be trusted to manage a line outside of a bathroom, but yet she hangs on year after year miss-managing many millions of your hard earned tax dollars. Why are we ok with this?

And on and on…

Most of the staff, engineers, web designers and other personnel have been omitted for now. It's not that they do not play a significant part in this drama, and you will find them sprinkled throughout this narrative where appropriate.

It is my belief that most of the staff is more than capable and eager to do their jobs as appropriate, even given the limitations that spiral down through the political quagmire. They suffer not from the inability to do their jobs, but from management's inability to direct them appropriately and effectively utilize the resources provided to them.

As far as technical training goes, the official line is that the state does not pay for actual training, but allows projects to be meandered through for long periods of time until it either barely works or until someone finally gives up and pays a large sum of money to someone to come fix the problem.

According to CZ, she sets the priorities of the agency and that most of the projects brought to the table are insignificant and will never be funded. Also according to CZ, all of the number one projects need to be managed and funded, but never are. CZ and JB fail to understand that you cannot have sixty or seventy number one priorities, and that it is better to begin and complete one job at a time rather than juggle five or six while dodging political landmines.

Most of the customers we purportedly are here to serve will more than likely be happy to go away and leave us alone once their place in the project schedule has been defined and communicated to them, but this is never the case and the frustration usually manifests itself though a carelessly crafted email to twenty or thirty thousand people. When people have realized that the only way to get a project done is to piss and moan to anyone who will listen until the director of the departments paranoia kicks in, something has gone very wrong.

Priorities should not be set by those seeking only to define themselves as excellent managers. The truth of the matter is that excellent managers are those who actually strive to achieve results to the benefit of those they serve.

Ignoring a project because it has no significant “me” factor is a waste of tax dollars and resources. Mandated projects are important, but no less important than the little projects that agencies require while providing a service to the public. If you are an agency intending to request a project from ITS, then you need to ask yourself the following questions before you walk into the project charter meeting.

“Will anyone outside of our agency actually notice if this project is not completed; is this project federally mandated; or finally, will substantial funds be lost if this project is not completed?” If there answer is no, your project will more than likely never make it off of the bottom of the list. If your project fails any of those questions, you are more than likely already screwed, but do bear with me and ask yourself one additional question: “Do I have enough clout to get this project in front of someone who can get those fuckers down in ITS to pay attention?” If the answer is no, then don’t waste your time.

As you read through these pages, please understand that although the pages you are reading represent my experience at DHS, it actually is in fact probably representative of government in general. We have pigeon-holed ourselves into processes and procedures that do not and never have made any sense.

Unfortunately, it’s about the politics and not the people who require these services, and the man or woman who finally figures out how to scrape the bullshit off the pile to reach the creamy nougat center is a man or woman we can truly call god-like in an agency clouded by self-preservation. Budgets are cut for essential services until a bridge collapses and then all of a sudden someone pulls the funding out of their ass to inspect the rest of the bridges. By the way, the new 35W bridge is REALLY nice.

As I continue this story, you will soon understand all of the things I told you that you would understand and quite a few more. You will most likely want to mail your congressman a copy of this book asking for oversight of this and all other agencies in the state organization. Please do, I need the money anyway.

But the bottom line is that you pay your taxes, and if you do not, they come and take your stuff, throw you in jail, or do whatever they need to do to get your tax dollars and therefore you damned well should have a right to ask for a reasonable level of accountability. If you go to the website for this book, there I have included all of the contact information for your representatives on my website goodenoughgov.com. Go forth and demand the things they promised you when they asked you to vote for them because they sure as hell are going to ask you to vote for them the next time.

CHAPTER 2
THE FALL GUY:

My career at DHS began pretty much as any other job begins on the first day. You show up, someone helps you find your desk, you take a picture for your badge, and then your manager walks you from person to person introducing you to everyone like you are the newest toy Chihuahua in their collection, and informing them of all the brilliant things you have done in your past life, and of all the brilliant things you are going to do in this one, and how happy they are to have you there.

I don't have an issue being the new toy Chihuahua, but while this might work in a small office, introducing you to sixty or seventy people in a large office is tantamount to asking me to count all of the beans in a five-gallon pail, and who gives a fuck anyway? At DHS, you are eventually going to run into almost everyone on one side of the fence or the other, and as far as friends vs. enemies, there isn't really a middle ground anywhere to be found.

By the time this was over, I had met about 40 or 50 people whose names I did not remember; figured out where the bathroom was; absorbed all of the fake smiles one could possibly stomach; and was pretty much hating myself, my past, and the fact that I had not yet won the lottery and was once again subject to this painful diatribe of discovery.

My first task was to attend the morning meeting with my staff and yet another round of introductions. This being slightly more manageable, I managed to pick up three or four more names, and get to repeat for myself my history, all of my great accomplishments, and tell everyone how happy I was to be there. By this time I was halfway between the proverbial god complex and halfway to slitting my wrists in absolute self-effacement, but what the hell, if this is how these things are done, then this is how we will do them.

> *Upon the completion of my self, one of my new engineers (SK) noticed the coffee cup in my hand and decided to lecture me on the fact that I was supporting the ivory towered corporate whores whose name rhymes with bar-bucks and suggested a local alternative instead.*

While in concept I can appreciate her enthusiasm in supporting local business, I can admit that I did not appreciate her intrusion into when and where I chose to spend my hard earned dollars, and not knowing me, nor knowing anything about me, it was truly and decidedly none of her fucking business.

However, being the gracious new manager I knew I could be, and instead of calling her the simplistic dingbat I inevitably deemed her to be, I simply explained to her that I had in fact been a regular customer of the particular local coffee house that she had recommended, and that after many years of steady patronage, they refused to resolve a health issue that I was concerned about and thus they had loss my business for that reason.

Besides, calling someone a simplistic dingbat on your first day is probably frowned upon and against union rules or something. I never checked. Maybe this was a test of the new manager, maybe not, but more on SK, soon to be SR later.

So having spent the first few hours of my day in a futile exercise in memory, I knew about 5 or 6 names and it was time to sit down with CZ to discuss all of the people I had just met.

I am pretty sure the preamble to this conversation included random verbalizations around her personal life, her cat, and the promise that I would never be bored due to all of the exciting things they would have going on for me… yada yada yada, which was immediately followed by, "Oh, yes, and we have some problems that you will quickly need to deal with once you get settled."

OK, here it comes. I have been in this job exactly 1 hour and I get thrown into the bucket of people they can't control, don't know what to do with, and can't fire so lets sic the new guy on them.

> "Of course, that's a good idea. If we get the new guy to do, it won't look like we were trying to skirt the rules at all. We can just say, hey, we hired a new manager and he changed the rules. No, no, no, not us, it was the new guy."

This is especially effective if one of the problem children is black, or "African American" for all of you politically correct fanatics, and the new manager is also black or "African American" – as I am for those of you politically correct lunatic fringe people who were about to burn this book and write out a check to the NAACP to apologize for the guilt you felt in simply reading this paragraph.

This brings us back to EC. You remember EC don't you? EC the engineering supervisor, African American, has been at DHS forever? Yeah, that's the one.

Anyway, the conversation went something like this and yes, I am paraphrasing for the sake of brevity and the non-existence of any sort of recording device in the room, which is apparently not allowed for some reason.

CZ: as I have explained, ITS has been around for quite a while, and over the years we have grown into quite a large organization. EC has been *around the whole time and been very good at helping us during this growth period, but...*

(There is always a but)

CZ: We have had some problems with his ability to manage projects and his customer interactions. Most of the customers don't like him because they feel that he does whatever he wants and doesn't meet their needs.

ME: Have you done anything about this?

CZ: Weeell, it's been difficult because I really needed him when I started because he was the only one who knew anything about the network and how it was configured. Things are done differently at the state. You can't just fire someone that easily, especially when they have been around for so long. (even if they are worthless) The other problem is that I have always given him above average reviews because I needed him, and he and I have developed a really good relationship.

ME: So is he doing any better?

CZ: Weeell, not really.

So here I am trying to understand her side of the picture, but also already looking around for a sharp knife to kill myself with.

As I have previously mentioned, the great thing about the private sector is that productivity is based on the bottom line, which is money. The other thing is that if someone does not perform, you can just fire his or her ass and be done with it. While I'll admit that a malicious individual, who either deems you to be a threat to their position or simply doesn't like you for any reason whatsoever, can also abuse this ability, it usually works out well if you are the employer with a slacker in your midst. Two hours into this position, I am already being told that I need to go forth and beat up on the little guy because she didn't have the balls to do it in the first place.

CZ spent the next hour or so explaining the relationships that exist between DHS ITS and the other agencies it supported; why these relationships were failing; and how it was pretty much EC's fault for being a crappy supervisor and a slacker. She also spent time explaining how PDs worked (position descriptions), how EDIs worked (employee reviews) and how the best thing for me to do would be do change (EC's) PD to set the expectations that she and now I would expect and that if I did not receive adequate response from this effort, that I needed to document absolutely everything that happened so that we could use it against him to remove him from his position.

Good Fucking God Batman… what had I walked into?

Before I get into how absolutely fucked I was already beginning to feel, I should point out that firing someone who works for the state, even with documentation, is an absolute pain in the ass and a full time job within itself, and that's the main reason it is rarely done and really shitty employees get to collect a pay check without actually producing anything.

The bottom line is that they hold all of the cards. If you look at them funny, they call their union rep and accuse you of creating a hostile environment. From that point on, you are the one being watched because apparently "you started it without any sort of provocation," and now they can say that you were after them from day one. This is not a good position to be in because inevitably they go around telling everyone how easy it was to bend you over a table, and anyone that you might happen to piss off in the future can do the same thing, citing the fact that you were already under investigation for the same thing a while back.

CZ and GO, of course, had dodged this bullet by hiring me and standing me in front of the firing squad. Any fucking idiot can see that the very second I walked into this situation, it became for me a no win situation. She was asking me to define the PD that she had not been able to define, require behavior that she had not been able to obtain, and most likely fire the employee if these benchmarks were not met. My asshole was already clenching in anticipation of the royal fucking it saw coming its way.

It also became quickly obvious that CZ defined all of the engineers as very good, but badly managed; unable to follow established policies and procedures, and unwilling to do so. CZ had effectively supported a supervisor who did whatever the hell he wanted, refused to share information, and could not manage to keep his direct reports on task because she with her limited technical background did not understand the infrastructure, pushed his priorities all over the place and was afraid to call EC on the carpet for fear of losing absolute control of the situation.

Keep in mind that this is the employee that for the previous six years that she had rated as "OUTSTANDING", on every EDI. I was already so irrevocably fucked that I could see into my own ass and that, my friends, is never, ever a good thing.

CZ then proceeded to tell me about problem child number two. SB was an engineer that had worked for ITS for about five years and had advanced to an engineer level four. CZ essentially told me in so many words, which were intermingled with stories about her grandchildren, that SB was a pain in the ass, was not liked by anyone, needed to go as soon as possible, and that it was my job to do it. This resulted in more clenching, and had I stood up at that moment, I would have taken the chair with me. In no uncertain terms, CZ informed me the bottom line was that SB's attitude and her way of dealing with people was harsh and disrespectful and that everyone had simply had enough.

I asked if anyone had attempted to work with her on her soft skills and was told the following:

> *"SB has had every opportunity to get her act together, we have talked to her over and over again and still gotten the same behavior." I was told that she (CZ) had many emails and much documentation from people who had worked with SB on projects and were upset or in one case of an employee that was no longer with DHS, that she was "afraid" of SB, and that I should talk to EC about the problems that they had had with her in the past."*

OK, so the obvious question, and one which I asked, was:

Me: If we have all of this documentation on her behavior why was she still here?

CZ: Well EC depends on her quite a bit. SB has always been his "go to" person when he needed something done.

Me: Is she a good engineer?

CZ: Well, I think in some ways, and I have to say that I personally like SB, but I don't see it. Part of being a good engineer is being able to communicate with customers and a very big part of this job is getting along with your peers. As far as I am concerned, she has had all of the opportunities she is going to get, and you need to document her behavior so we can get rid of her.

The fourth thing that she told me was that although my title was "Architectural & Engineering Manager," the Architect NB would continue to report to her for the time being. According to her, "It would just be easier until I get my feet wet," but the actual truth was that by keeping that control under her thumb, she either didn't trust me, or simply wanted to maintain control at the highest level of her recently built, but currently crumbling empire. This was just fucking getting better and better all the time.

The rest of the conversation was spent with her explaining all of the damaged relationships between all of the other agencies and the responsibilities of GO who was a contractor hired when DHS designed and built it's shiny new datacenter in downtown St. Paul, and from whom I would be taking my guidance. WTF?

Also, I mention the following only to preface my partial, but immediate dislike of GO.

IT IS AGAINST STATE LAW FOR CONTRACTORS TO MANAGE STATE EMPLOYEES.

I say partial dislike because while I may have been a bit presumptuous in not liking him in the first place, his lack of personality and Neanderthal like people skills immediately filled in the remaining slots of dislike quite nicely.

As explained by CZ, the agencies with which ITS had bad relationships were:

"SOS" because we were ordered to integrate their systems into ours and they don't want to do that. This has been going on for more than five years.

"SSIS" which is run by a tyrant who hates EC and feels that because their agency runs and is paid for by federal subsidies, they feel like they are special and don't have to do what we tell them to do.

"OET" which has the governor's permission to run the entirety of the statewide technical infrastructure, but doesn't know enough about all of the individual agencies to take it over so all of the agencies keep doing their own thing under the radar. I was also told that under no circumstances was I to provide any information to OET without running it by her first.

"CSED" which is run by a quite different tyrant who for some reason doesn't like CZ and works under the radar until caught. (I had my ideas about why they don't like CZ, but I digress for the moment).

OK, so lets do a quick recap here folks. I'm three hours into my first day and my first four tasks are as follows.

> *1: Document the shortcomings of an employee that she has officially labeled in writing and in power and responsibility as outstanding so that this employee can actually provide this*

"OUTSTANDING" service as she requires, OR, figure out a way to remove the employee from his position.

2: Document the shortcomings of a second employee who seems to be the one engineer on the team who is one of the few employees that can consistently be counted on to complete complicated tasks when time is of the essence, so that she can be fired as quickly as possible.

3: Utilize current policies and procedures to get the Engineering team to be more productive and responsive to our customers. It should be noticed at this point that these policies and procedures have been in existence for more than five years and have not been effective, but that I was told that these are the policies and procedures that needed to be used and that any changes needed to be run by her first.

4: Repair years of damaged relationships between agencies due to lack of responsiveness, bad management, and passive aggressive politicking.

5: DO IT ALL PRETTY MUCH BEFORE LUNCH.

Despite the fact that my keen sense of survival was kicking me in the ass urging me to run, not walk, to the nearest exit and call the other company that had offered me a position, I assured CZ that I would do my best to implement her desires and get to the bottom of the well of technical despair she had managed to design. I noted that the first thing I would do would be to talk to the staff (especially my two problem children) to determine the best way to handle the situations which I had been given. And that I would meet with GO as soon as possible to get more history on the agency because apparently his shit doesn't stink, and research the agency, its employees and the best way to handle each of these tasks and report back to her.

I returned to my office, scheduled a meeting with each of my staff for the next day, checked email, and fought back the pain of disillusionment that was quickly building in my chest.

I also find it quite amusing that for at least a month or so, every morning when I walked in the door, CZ's first statement was "Oh, wow, you came back." On reflection, I should have been asking myself if this was her way of seeing if my initial level of interest had been stifled by the obviously grueling and possibly illegal tasks I had been saddled with. It is one thing to be asked by your new boss to run a marathon, and quite another to have a 12 pound bowling ball handed to you just before the starting pistol is fired. I had been handed no less than four of them.

In the afternoon, I was handed off to GO for a review of the agency, and all of its particular projects, pitfalls and issues that came with the job. GO had been asked to manage EC as well, but it was quickly obvious that EC had pretty much told him to fuck off and the first hour or so was permeated with conversation about EC's behavioral issues and the fact that he needed to be gone as soon as possible.

GO and I spent the next several hours talking about the fifty or so projects that were outstanding and all of the difficulties they were having getting these project completed (according to him, mostly due to EC's incompetent management style).

Most of the reasons for the failure of these projects centered around:

The fact that EC was a lousy supervisor and refused to cooperate because he was jealous of GO's authority and the absolute power that GO had been granted by CZ.

The fact that EC relied on SB for most of his projects and the fact that apparently absolutely no one liked SB meant that projects meandered along in absolute futility until enough people jumped up and down and screamed. This also meant that ITS was usually operating in reactive mode and would thus take exorbitant amounts of time to complete projects because the engineers were constantly being bounced around from project to project.

He also reiterated CZ's assertion that if OET were to learn enough about our agency, they would come over here and take over so that I had to be very careful with regard to what I told them about us. I was commanded that absolutely no technical information was to be relayed to them and I was also warned in no uncertain terms that if contacted by OET, I was not to meet with them or discuss any DHS issues unless he was present.

I am sure you can imagine that by now I am feeling an innate sense of paranoia, wondering whom to trust, and trying to figure out if this was all a complete bullshit exercise in self preservation (which we all now know it was) or if the actual truth was that given a chance, everyone who worked for the state was not to be trusted and would stab you in the back to make themselves look better. This usually turned out to be also true.

GO talked about how he had had no success in getting EC to cooperate with his mandates and that EC would play the passive aggressive role and simply disappear when confronted with anything he deemed uncomfortable, which was pretty much everything. We talked about what a pain in the ass SB was, but that she was the person EC relied on most to complete projects, and that it was imperative that we keep her in the background of all projects so as not to irritate the customers.

This went on for several hours, and I have to say that by this time my sense of self was waning. These fuckers had not brought me in to manage an engineering department. These fuckers had brought me in to deal with all of the bullshit that they had previously failed at dealing with and to take the fall should the shit hit the fan.

I was, within my first hours of my first day, being offered up as the sacrificial lamb and there was no way in hell that I was going to get out of it. This had all been planned out in advance, and I could already feel the rope tightening around my balls and the trap door loosening.

CZ had told me that there had been several internal applications for this position, but that she felt someone from the outside would be better. Of course, it would take an outsider to take a bullet for the team. An insider would already know the ropes and would have told them to go fuck themselves in the worst way. There was absolutely no way an already vetted state employee was going to step into this shit, and there would be nothing CZ could do about it if they refused. NB later told me that this bullshit was exactly the reason he hadn't wanted the position.

So it had to be an outsider. It had to be someone who could step, however carefully, through the mine field and would be able to take all of the shrapnel when one of those landmines exploded and could brush it all off as a newbie error. It had to be someone who was new and fresh, full of new ideas and public sector vim, and it was going to be me.

Truth be told, I needed the job, I needed the money, and I actually at this point, still wanted to make a difference. I promised myself that I wasn't going to become one of those zombie eyed state employees who did nothing very well and got paid even better for it. I was indeed going to make a difference. Please feel free to take a moment for laughter if you need to.

I was going to bring twenty years of IT experience to a department that had been in existence for less than 10. I was going to turn this department around and I was going to resolve all of the problems that had been presented to me efficiently and expeditiously.

And I was going to do it without fucking anyone over, by establishing fantastic relationships with the other agencies, and by showing the rest of the state agencies how an efficient and productive IT team should work. I was going to do it my way, and I was going to do it without firing anyone.

This is where I get to ask the following question: "How fucking deluded was I?" I was already dead, only I just didn't know it yet.

I didn't know that everyone thought that CZ was an inept lunatic who was in way over her head and had no concept of how to run an IT department. I also didn't know that she kept those close to her who were for whatever reasons willing to bend to her ideologies and paranoia and I did feel that I could deal with the "in over her head thing," but the paranoia was another issue all together.

I am constantly reminded of the saying that “just because you’re paranoid, it doesn’t mean they aren’t all out to get you.” They were actually all out to get me, and it was only my first day.

The next several days went by relatively quickly. I met a bunch more people, listened to the rants and raves, and met with CZ to learn more about the agency, her cat, the dock in the lake behind her house, who to trust and not to trust, why everyone hates ITS, yada yada yada. I had a headache going home every day and quite simply put, I was beginning to want my mommy.

I also began the series of meetings that I had scheduled with each of my direct reports. I had sent them an additional message after my first one asking them to provide me with a list of issues they might wish to discuss. With only one exception, EC of course, they all came prepared to discuss the things on their minds.

EC indicated that he was quite happy with his position and had no concerns. (Of course he had no concerns. He did whatever the fuck he wanted and dared them to challenge him.) He answered all of my questions with one or two words, and refused to elaborate on anything I decided to delve into. I understood his hesitancy. I was the new guy and most people are hesitant to trust the new guy. I would deal with that later.

There was an interesting moment where he managed to spit out an actual complete sentence. He told me in no uncertain terms that he had assembled a great team, that they all worked well together, (this was not necessarily true) and that changing anything in the way he did things would be a really bad idea. This was also not necessarily true.

For each of these meetings with my new team, I began each meeting exactly the same – asking them to tell me about their experience, particular technical specialties, background, and what they liked and disliked about their jobs.

All of them said pretty much the same thing except for SB who essentially called me an idiot and questioned my ability to do the job. I would deal with that later as well. The rest of them indicated that they wanted their department to be more organized, that they wanted the projects they were working on to be managed better, that they were tired of being juggled from job to job, and that they hated working with SB.

Of course, none of them actually mentioned her name, but I had received enough of that from everyone else I had met to understand just whom they were talking about. Hell, I was beginning to hate this woman myself and I had only just met her once at the morning meeting. I had saved her interview for last.

So to recap once again… every one hates working for EC and thinks he is a bad manager who is unable to organize his staff. Everyone hates SB and only worked with her because EC made them, and all of our customers thought we were inept, worthless idiots. I knew that I had my work cut out for me.

And then I met SB. SB, late 40s, articulate, old school country girl, big smile and eyes that scan the scene as if they are looking for something to pounce on. Oh, yeah, I have met one of these before. Keeping in mind that everyone I had met over the last few days told me what a pain in the ass she was, I already knew that there was nothing I could tell this woman. This was strictly an information-gathering mission, and she was the one doing the gathering.

I dove in, asking the standard "tell me about you and your job" questions and she fired back answers and quite a few questions. (She was the only one who did this.) This woman had something to prove. She answered my questions as asked and pulled no punches. This was a woman who had something to prove and wasn't shy about it.

I listened respectfully, keeping in mind the things I had been told, but determined to keep my promise to myself and go in with an open mind. I asked questions, and she answered them. She asked questions, and I answered them. After about an hour and a half of this, I could see what everyone was saying, she was indeed a pain in the ass.

But here's the catch. SB was probably only a pain in the ass if you were one of those people more concerned with self preservation than with succeeding on your own merits. I had already figured out by the generic bullshit answers the rest of them gave that it wasn't really about her being a pain in the ass, but more about her not falling in line behind the rest of the state ITS sheep.

You asked a question of SB, you got an answer, and it really didn't matter if it wasn't the answer you wanted. It was the answer and usually the right one.

If you asked a question of CZ, you got a bullshit passive aggressive convoluted diatribe about the complexities of government and how we needed to be careful when making decisions because everything is under scrutiny.

If you asked a question of EC, you got a mumbled and looping tangle of unrelated and confusing technical information with no relation to each other to further confuse the issue.

If you asked GO a question, you got a running narrative of how great he was and several reminders of the fact that CZ trusted him implicitly, along with the fact that he more than likely would have your balls in a sling if you crossed him in any way whatsoever.

I soon realized that the truth isn't necessarily a state requirement for employment. Self-preservation is, and the constant "under scrutiny" line from CZ was bullshit, because if they were to actually scrutinize the ITS agency and the way it does business, I am pretty sure federal charges would be quickly forthcoming.

I decided right then and there that I liked SB. She reminded me much of myself. Hard core, no bullshit, go-getter and people don't always like that. Well, fuck them and the horse they rode in on. I made up my mind then and there that not only was I not going to fire SB, I was going to take her under my wing and teach her how to "manage people."

I was going to teach her how to get things done. I was supposed to be good at this shit after all. I had been doing it for twenty years, and one of the major things you learn in twenty years is that not only do you not take anyone else's shit, you convince them to eat yours and like it. It's not about being careful not to step on toes on your way up the corporate ladder, it's about teaching those who own the toes you step on to appreciate the pain. Yeah, this was going to be easy.

Now, you do realize that my conversation with SB would not have been complete, and I would have been ignoring my duties, if I had not brought up the fact that everyone hated her. It had to be done. I had to hear the other side of the story from the other side of the bridge.

If there is anything that my ex-wife taught me after I kicked her sorry ass out of the house it is that there are always three sides of every story. There is always his, hers, and the truth. Of course, I shall not delve into the delusional state of mind of my ex wife where the truth has never actually resided, but I digress, as that is another book entirely.

And so I jumped in with both feet.

> *"As you know, over the last few days, I have met with everyone in the department, as well as the other managers. It has been suggested by more than one of them that there seem to be problems working with you."*

SB was immediately in tears and I was digging through my cabinets in search of tissues.

We talked for over an hour. She explained to me the history of ITS, of her friendship with EC, how other people resented this friendship, or simply did not understand it, etc. She also mentioned that she was and always had been the one who led the projects to conclusion at EC's direction. She suggested that quite possibly this was the reason others resented her.

It became immediately clear that she did not, could not, and maybe even was not capable of understanding the severity of the situation she was in. I, of course, had to stick to the most obvious conclusion, which was that if forty people tell me that you are a pain in the ass, then you are quite probably, most likely a pain in the ass – be it intentional or not.

So I asked her: "So, how would you suggest I handle this situation?"

She responded with the following suggestion: removing her from EC's direct supervision and allowing her to work on projects outside of that group would most likely resolve the problem. This was already a problem because as they say, "no man (or woman) is an island." She needed those people, whether she wanted to acknowledge it or not.

I didn't realize that it wasn't that she wanted to work on her own, but that she wanted to be in charge of those people. This was another issue to be dealt with later. We talked for a while, the tears continued to flow, and I assured her that I would come up with a solution. For the moment, you have to realize that at this point SB is claiming that she was the victim and that all she wanted to do was her job in the best way possible.

OK, so now I have yet another person who implies that EC's management style left much to be desired, and I absolutely hated the circle of emotional bullshit and infighting that seemed to be the norm at DHS. The next issue, of course, is that now I have to go to EC to see what his take on SB's behavior is.

The other issue here is that there are very specific rules regarding what you can, and what you cannot do to employees for anything that might be considered of a disciplinary nature. The one thing you are able to do, as long as you do not "take anything away from them," is change their job or to whom they report. After that it gets a bit bumpy, but so be it. After all, I was still under the illusion that this was going to be an easy fix. And off I ran to speak to EC.

EC immediately took offense that I had gotten involved with one of his direct reports and stated in no uncertain terms that if I was going to go after SB, when she filed a lawsuit against the state, he was going to be on her side. I found this to be a bit disconcerting to say the least.

There was no reasoning with him. He knew the rules far better than I did and was going to make damned sure I knew who was in charge, and as far as he was concerned, it wasn't me.

It wasn't enough that I explained to him that it was not my goal to "manage his people," as he put it, but simply to offer advice and guidance. Informing him that CZ had some concerns with regard to his performance, he became very quiet. I spent the next ten minutes trying to get him to talk about why everyone was telling me that he was not a good manager and provided little guidance. He only wanted to know who had said that and little else. Of course, I would not give him this information.

Finally, I told him that I needed to go and would grab him later to continue this conversation. He reluctantly agreed with all the enthusiasm of a battered child, and so I just said the hell with it and told him that I was taking SB as my direct report, but that once things were cleared up he could have her back. He said little if anything, but only stared into his computer monitor.

CZ had told me that when EC is feeling threatened he goes into passive aggressive mode and disappears. He did just that and I did not see him for the rest of the day. At the time, I thought that was funny. That funny feeling wouldn't last very long at all, and it very quickly started to piss me off.

I went back to speak with CZ regarding my conversations with SB & EC. I informed her that I did not think that her faith in EC was well placed and that he was not on her side as she thought. I told her about the fact that even though she had been allowing EC to deal with all of the issues that had occurred over the years with SB, he had stated in no uncertain terms that SB had many things that she could sue the state for, and that if this were to occur, he would be on her side. CZ told me that she found this hard to believe, since he had been involved in all of the complaints and had been collecting information on these issues. This bitch was so irrevocably deluded about what was going on in her department that it was getting pretty scary from my point of view.

I told CZ that, yes, it was true that EC had a folder containing all of the complaints, but that he had simply handed them to SB for review and then immediately done nothing about them past that.

We talked for quite a while, and it became quite apparent that she was not going to take any of this into consideration in forcing me to deal with these issues and that the bottom line was that I was expected to begin the process from the beginning and find a way to get rid of SB and to make EC do his job.

The truth be told, I didn't get it. You have an individual who is not doing his job, but for some reason remains under your protection. You have another individual who isn't doing her job, and even though your biggest desire is to see this person walked out of the door, you take no action, complain incessantly about it, and then pass the buck to someone who doesn't know the system, the people or the processes. Yeah, I knew right then and there that I was truly, irrevocably fucked and I was about to take that bullet for the team in the worst place possible.

Over the next few months, SB did indeed turn out to be more and more of a pain in the ass, and I quickly realized that she was already about as screwed as I was about to be. No one was going to help her out of this because at the state there is no reason whatsoever to stick your neck out for anyone. You would be tolerated and little else, or you would be marginalized until you with quit or did something so incredibly stupid that they had no choice but to fire you. In a way, SB and I became fuck buddies and not at all in the good way.

While working for the State of Minnesota, the prospect of actually losing your job is an iffy prospect at best because there are at least a gazillion ways you can dispute any disciplinary action through your union. From that point on, almost any thing that is done to you, no matter how minor and even if it is for the good of the state, looks malicious and retaliatory, so no one bothers to get rid of the slackers. You simply fall into a black hole, where you can reside quite happily until you retire. And thus you should always remember the number one rule of thumb when working for the state:

Self-preservation is king, performance is secondary, and never, ever go out on a limb for anyone unless you have an escape plan and an absolute way of explaining away your loyalty to whatever head happens to be on the chopping block.

And so during the next several months, I worked with my apparent subordinates, peers and management to attempt to learn the ropes at DHS. The ropes, as it were, have all of the cohesiveness of an M.C. Escher painting. CZ seemed incredibly surprised that I actually returned to work every morning and this in itself is telling. When the person who interviewed you and convinced you to take a job is surprised that you actually show up every morning, it tends to lead you to only one viable conclusion: that you in fact are fodder for whatever evil plan that happens to be ongoing; that she lied to you in order to get you to take the job, and that at some point you are going to have to decide to either become one of the mindless automatons, or bail back into the pool of unemployment.

I am sure that those of you who happen to work for the state have all at one point promised yourself that you would never, ever, become one of them. Unfortunately, one day you woke up and realized that you had in fact become one of them, and that having stayed this long, it only made sense that you stuck it out for the long haul.

As I was saying, I worked with my subordinates and my peers learning the ropes. It became extremely apparent that even those who appeared to want to work with each other, none of them trusted each other. BG specifically gave me a list of people who were not to be trusted, most of whom were from other agencies and who were our customers. All of us, especially GO, were under explicit orders to keep infrastructure information internal only, even when it was obvious that dissemination of this information would serve to enhance the services that we provided to other agencies.

CZ decided that I was literate enough to represent the agency on public projects, although all information was to be filtered through her and GO and to be kept on a need to know basis. GO and I spent several afternoons going over the projects that were on the list, with detailed information on why these projects would be handled by ITS, but that the level of cooperation would be determined by ITS and not the requesting agency.

CZ immediately involved me in participating in all of the projects where ITS was to appear to be cooperating, if only in spirit, but it was obvious that my role was more that of a spy than that of an actual representative of the agency. A detailed report was expected at the conclusion of each of these meetings, and detailed instructions on how I was expected to respond to any questions of issues was given before the next meeting so that she could instruct me on how to respond to any issues.

CZ and GO were especially paranoid that OET, given enough information about our infrastructure, would exercise its authority over the state technical architecture and assume control over the ITS network and its staff. I did not see what the problem was, as it seemed to me that a combination of technologies statewide would only serve to reduce costs and increase coordination of efforts between all state agencies. As you are no doubt aware by now, this isn't really the goal of ITS management staff, and most of the energy is obviously spent maintaining the secretive well of self-preservation.

EC continued his practice of passive aggressiveness and made himself scarce if he thought that I was actually looking for him. SB continued to work on projects that I assigned to her and made relatively good progress on them. It was difficult for me to understand exactly what her motivation was in performing her job or in her dealings with her peers. It became obvious that she was in fact very manipulative and tried to maintain control under the guise of "following the rules." The thing about working for an agency that has very specific rules to be followed is that they can either work for you or against you, and the people at ITS were very accomplished at using those rules to their advantage. This would become apparent in many of the projects that SB and EC were involved with.

An example of this is that SB considered herself to be the lead engineer at DHS due to her relationship with EC and because of her length time there. DHS engineers rank from level one to five with five being the highest. SB was a four, but because EC had always relied on her to come to his rescue, level no longer mattered to her. She usually referred to the rest of the engineers as "her engineers", and quickly became quite upset if a project began that she was not the lead on or involved in some managerial way. The problem here was obvious, as her way of dealing with this particular dilemma was to send the offending engineer an email requesting all information on the project and to inform them that all decisions regarding this project should be and should have been run through her before starting. Another email would follow to EC demanding to know why this project was authorized without consulting her first. Obviously, this would start an uncomfortable series of emails between all involved usually resulting in the offending engineer removing him or herself from the conversation by requesting that SB pretty much piss off.

If a project that SB considered herself in charge of was not going her way, she would quote rules and specifications that the project was obviously not following in order to derail the project. If there was a website that was to be created in one security zone, SB would find a justification to explain why it needed to reside in another security zone and would fire off an email to two separate security teams who would then begin a series of meetings to determine which security zone the website should reside in. Security people are by nature paranoid, obsessive individuals in the first place; when you combine this paranoia with a passive aggressive sense of self-preservation, you get a cluster fuck of non-action. Ideally, while all of this activity is going on, I would have had an engineer build the web server so that it could be dropped into whatever security zone was eventually decided on. But this is not how it works. Inevitably, all work stops until that decision is made, and only then continues. The problem is that the decision is never actually made, thousands of dollars of equipment sit on the shelf, and customers get more and more pissed off about it. Two years later, the equipment is considered outdated, the customer demands new equipment, and the process starts all over again.

At this point, I would usually end up in EC's office asking him the history of the project, why a particular engineer was assigned to the project, who is the best person for the project, yada yada, yada. Two things quickly became obvious. SB did not quite understand that I was allowing EC to make decisions regarding the project assignments because he was their supervisor and micro-management is not really my style, and that EC was punishing SB for my removal of her from his supervision and generally treating her like shit in the process.

For the two issues, there were two obvious solutions, but since it was almost impossible to fire them, no matter what CZ wanted, I had to come up with alternatives. Believe me when I say that by this point, I really wanted to fire them both. They were both incredible pains in my ass, and I had come to realize that if I fired EC I could have managed his direct reports directly and gotten more done in much shorter periods of time. While SB was turning out to be a decent engineer, her people skills sucked the big one, and I was already spending too much time trying to convince her that you catch more flies with honey than vinegar and shielding her from the customers who found her abrasive attitude less than tolerable no matter how good of an engineer she was.

She was increasingly and completely of the opinion that if you pull the wings off those flies that they will drink whatever the fuck you give them, and she wasn't budging on this methodology. EC on the other hand would simply choose to continue to nurture his sense of self-entitlement and wait until the storm blew over.

This whole situation was seriously beginning to suck ass, but I realized that there was going to be only one option. CZ informed me that it was my job to teach EC how to manage people rather than manage them myself. I believed that it was my job to coordinate effort in order to keep projects moving forward and not to babysit a 46 year old man who acted like a child and retreated to his room when things didn't go his way.

Whatever instruction I could give him would be futile given the fact that I would tell him something, and then upon my next meeting with CZ I would be told that he had been bending her ear stating that I needed to let him work his own way and not manage “his” people. The kicker here is that she blew smoke up his ass, told him that he was right, and that she would talk to me. She would then tell me that I needed to teach him better methods for managing “his” people. The problem, as I saw it, was that when I went to his people and asked them to do something, it got done. When he went to them and sliced and diced them from project to project to project, they fucked around for extended periods of time achieving nothing.

In the meanwhile, I assigned SB to specific projects over which I had direct control in order to keep track of both the projects and her relationship with customers. As I stated before, SB was a very competent engineer, but was lacking in any sort of soft skills. I use the term competent in lieu of a more appropriate term because although SB was not certified in any of the areas she professed expertise in, extensive periods of trial and error as well as time spent working with these particular technologies at DHS afforded her a reasonable knowledge of them. She worked diligently to solve whatever problems I presented to her, and with considerable urging from me, she even managed to include those more knowledgeable than she in these areas. This was a great step forward as far as I was concerned, however it quickly became apparent to me that no matter how diligently she worked on these projects, those who had been involved with her over the years were less than willing to give her an opportunity to prove her usefulness. Forgiveness was also not a prerequisite to working together at DHS and was in fact was pretty much non-existent.

CZ continued to make no secret of the fact that her plate of things to do was over loaded and that I needed to get up to speed in order to relieve her workload. It was my most secret desire, as well as everyone else's, to tell her that if she would simply shut the fuck up about all of the bullshit in her personal life and coordinate her own efforts, her plate would be considerably less crowded. I doubt if she would have listened to this coming from me or from anyone else, but the dream of being able to inform someone of his or her shortcomings is always a difficult one to quiet.

CZ explained all of the relationships with other agencies that would most likely need repairing, but cautioned me not to trust any of the other agencies and to make sure to run all conversations I might have with them by her to ensure I didn't step on any landmines.

The practical translation of this is that her paranoia was in full swing and that she was concerned that I would provide information to the other agencies that would subvert her priorities and sense of self-preservation.

An example of this would be the incredibly damaged relationship she had developed with the Projects Management Office (PMO). She told me that I would need to work with them to build up trust because EC had destroyed it over the years by not being able to respond to their needs in an efficient manner. The PMO office is tasked with managing state projects from inception to completion.

The problem with this is that the PMO office has no technical staffing and yet sustains an overwhelming desire to manage ITS projects. You will read more detailed information on this in the chapter about all of the projects that I worked on, but the gist of the matter is that every agency is more concerned with its viability than it is concerned with the minor detail of actually understanding the problem and possible solutions.

I made an appointment with TS who was in charge of the PMO office project managers. TS was also anxious to meet me and greeted me by telling me that it was "so good to see another "brother" in DHS management. I like to see minorities climb the corporate ladder as well, however I didn't really care whether or not he felt that "brothers" were given a fair shake in state government. Another reason that I found this so interesting was that a few days before that, CZ stopped me in the hallway to extol my virtues and tell me how happy everyone was that I was there. She also stated the following:

> *CZ: "I shouldn't be telling you this, but everyone really likes you. In fact, someone stopped me yesterday to tell me how good you were and told me that they weren't aware that I had a disparity in my department." She followed up by stating that she hoped that this did not offend me.*

The State of Minnesota uses the term disparity to define a lack of one thing or another that fails to meet certain legal criteria. This person was basically saying that the reason I was hired was because I was African American, and it couldn't possibly have been for any other reason. The truth of the matter is that I was offended as hell, but I maintained my composure. Did she think that idiotic racist comments were something new to me? And if she did, why would she bother telling me this in the first place? This also served to increase my belief that one of the main reasons she had hired me was so that if we were able to discover a way to remove EC from his position, it would look so much better if it were black man to do the deed for her. Of course, she had already irrevocably fucked that up by giving him excellent reviews over the last five years, and I had no plans on becoming her token "hit" bitch.

And so I met with TS, who immediately launched into an obviously prepared twenty-minute diatribe about how important it was for us to work together and how anxious they were be involved in our projects. I listened to this for a while nodding in all of the right places, and adding the affirmative grunt here and there where he would have been expecting them. It wasn't that I had any reason to doubt his sincerity, except for the fact that over the years I have sat in enough meetings with vendors and customers to recognize a sales pitch when I heard one.

TZ wasn't interested in serving ITS in any capacity whatsoever. This was plain and simply the other side of the power struggle and another attempt to build an empire. He also indicated that there had been quite a bit of bad blood between ITS and PMO, and that he wasn't sure how this had happened. It was all I could do to not tell him that the reasons were not as complex as he supposed them to be. I wanted to tell him that the reason there was so much bad blood between them was because his office and CZ's office were acting like two fucking three year olds fighting over a toy.

I listened to TS ramble on about how interested they were in managing our projects, made notes, and evaluated his level of sincerity, which was losing ground with every word. The thing you have to understand about technology is that in general it's pretty simple. Forget all of the speculative and secretive bullshit that you have heard over the years, technology is no more complex than baking a cake. That is to say that a series of ingredients appropriately measured out and assembled in the right order serve to produce an end result. Either you put in the time and effort to learn all of the components and how they work together, or you don't. It was quite obvious that TS and his group had not bothered, and the end result would be the same as if you placed all of the ingredients for an elaborate triple creamcheese, chocolate cake on my kitchen counter. There is a reasonable chance that whatever I come up with might be edible, but the chances are just as great that it's going to be complete shit as I am not a baker.

Having listened for almost an hour, I told TS that, being the new guy on the block, I was happy to work with him and his group on ITS projects, but that my concern was their ability to manage ITS projects, given that none of them were trained in technology or even certified in Project Management. I told TS that one of the ways that we could get around these issues was that the PMO could be responsible for the overall initiatives put forth by DHS, but that ITS would be responsible for the technology portion of these projects. I told him that in this way we could ensure that the technology portion of all state projects would be completed correctly and that adequate costs, timelines, and expectations could be set for their overall projects. He agreed, and after about another half hour or so of working of the details, we parted and I assured him that I would present our new proposal to CZ. I left feeling some sense of accomplishment and thinking that I had put a stick in the ground with regard to repairing some of the bad history. This feeling was short lived, as it took CZ about 90 seconds to destroy any sense of accomplishment I had managed to acquire.

I sat down with CZ and went over the details of my conversation with TS. I told her that we had agreed that the PMO would manage the overall projects and turn over the technology portion to ITS for management. Her immediate and unequivocal response was "absolutely not".

> *CZ: "we will not be cooperating with them on any projects. I have tried to work with TS before, and if he wants any cooperation from us, he is going to have to come see me first."*

ME: "I don't understand. We have agreed that we would manage the ITS portion of the projects and that they would manage the rest. What's the problem?"

CZ: You don't understand the history, so you should just let me handle this. If TS wants to work with us, then he is going to have to come work it out with me."

OK, so this bitch sent me into the lion's den to figure out a way for our two agencies to cooperate and then decides that any agreement between us would have to be negotiated between her and them. It was becoming obvious. She didn't want a cooperative environment between agencies. She wore the keys to the kingdom around her fat little neck, and she wanted you to kiss her ass in order to gain access to them. There wasn't going to be any cooperative environment, and I wasn't going to kiss her ass. It was her way or the highway, as those of us who had to deal with her inevitably found out, and it was a very long and horribly bumpy, cellulite-infested highway. So what was the fucking point of sending me over there in the first place then?

Over the next several weeks, I continued to meet with managers from other agencies in futile attempts to repair damage that I didn't create and apparently didn't understand well enough to be trusted with and all with similar results. CZ didn't really seem to want to work with them. What she wanted was absolute power, and apparently she had achieved it by denying services to those who needed them. The question I had was how did someone with such obviously high levels of paranoia and no obvious technology knowledge obtain and keep control of such a large state agency's technology division? As I mentioned previously, everyone I spoke to considered her a complete fucking whacko in immediate need of therapy, but as I also mentioned, it is a complete and absolute pain in the ass to fire someone from there once they have achieved tenure, so they simply don't bother, and these people are allowed to lord over millions of your tax dollars while allowing essential services to flounder.

To explain the illogical nature of this, I will provide an example. Management expects weekly reports from CZ to show progress on specific high-level projects. By high-level, I mean projects that someone in upper management will notice. Someone in the PMO created specific forms for reporting on these projects, and CZ emailed these forms to us.

The structure of these forms had been changed several times, and each time it was emailed to us from CZ. At our weekly managers meeting, CZ printed out the completed reports and immediately started screaming and yelling about how we had done the forms wrong and that we had used the incorrect forms, as well as how upset JB was when she had to go to a meeting with the wrong forms. We pointed out to CZ that we had used the latest forms that she has sent us, and she spent the next ten minutes screaming about how she had embarrassed herself to upper management.

Somewhere in her head, she made the conscious decision to review her outgoing emails. As we all sat around the table feeling like scolded children, she figured out that we had in fact used the latest version of the forms that she had sent us. Under normal circumstances, I would have expected her to concede her error, however, this wasn't her way. She simply informed us again that we had used the wrong form, and that we would have to do them over again. This is the sort of logic that was indicative of her management style. It never mattered that you were right. You were always wrong, it was usually someone else that was angry because of it, and she was just relaying the information to us from those that had apparently somehow been wronged by our stupidity. A week later, we had completed the reports again and were informed that they would have to be done over again because the information was landscape and not horizontal. Apparently, “it was too much work for JB to have to turn the pages to the side in order to read them.” Of course, we were told that “JB was furious” because someone had stopped her in the hallway, and she had to fumble with the reports in order to give them an answer to the question. The forms were then re-designed, but at least this time she sent us the correct ones.

Anyway, it became apparent that at DHS, being told to solve a problem doesn’t necessarily mean that the person doing the requesting actually wants the problem solved, but rather they value the propriety that admiring the problem presents. Being the official DHS sacrificial lamb, or as you are all now aware, the DHS token African American manager, I continued to be sent to agency after agency to come up with a solution to years of mistrust only to be told that the only way these problems were going to be resolved was if the appropriate management from those agencies were to bend over in front of CZ for a royal fucking. Because I had been the one to present solutions to these agencies and promised to make them work, my credibility quickly turned to shit when the cooperation I had promised them failed to materialize. But I kept going to those agencies because that was my job according to CZ, and someone needed to do it. What was actually happening was that I was plain and simply a spy for DHS and should have had no expectations of any sort of success in these endeavors.

In the meanwhile, I continued to attempt to manage EC’s inordinately confusing sense of project management, SB’s highly overwhelming sense of entitlement, and GO’s sense of absolute domination over the staff.

EC had finally figured out that if he simply gave me what I wanted and kept me informed on the status of all projects he was tasked with, I pretty much left him to his own devices. Don't get me wrong, he still played as many games as ever and utilized the system to his benefit as much as possible. It was difficult to know where things stood, as he somehow managed to keep everything jumbled up in his head.

The only effective way to deal with this was to keep sending him back until you got what you wanted. For example, in order to keep track of what he was working on and ordering for those particular projects, I simply informed purchasing that I needed to see all purchase requisitions before they approved them. This meant that he would not be able to complete a project without my pre-approval. He had a nasty habit of mixing up projects in order to keep us off guard and unaware of what was being purchased. The net effect was that he got to order toys for one project and then use them as he saw fit in another. Several months later, he would bring the second part of the project in for approval as part of another purchase order saying that this was the second part of the original project. Unless you have a computer for a brain, it became impossible to keep track of it all. By requiring him to submit all of the components of a project before it would be approved, we attempted to ensure that the purchases were going to their intended project.

There were also rumors as to what actually happened to servers once he deemed them out of service. He tended to want to replace equipment even when it was functioning perfectly. One rumor, which was relayed to me by BG, was that a pallet of servers in his care simply disappeared from the dock with no explanation whatsoever. Now in the private sector, if a pallet of servers turned up missing, all sorts of hell would break loose. Inquiries would be held, polygraphs mandated, and someone's head would eventually roll off that very same dock where the servers had disappeared. Not so at DHS. No one seemed to give a fuck and the missing servers were simply added to the list of inventory items to be tracked down and put back in the drawer.

To further explain this point, I was once presented with a list of equipment that purchasing was unable to account for. I believe that the equipment on this list totaled somewhere just shy of one million dollars, and no matter how many people I asked, not one individual seemed interested in locating this missing equipment. Perhaps it was because of the futility of trying to chew your way though the bullshit and bureaucracy, or perhaps because actually inquiring into such misbehavior usually results in you getting your ass chewed out by your manager for sticking your finger in something that was not under your purview. Simply put, you do not ask too many questions that might open that proverbial can of worms in which someone up the ladder would be looking for an explanation, and you might have to explain why you never investigated it in the first place. So things like that were completely ignored.

EC's management style still left a great deal to be desired, but he had decided that he wasn't going to change, I couldn't fire him, and any disciplinary actions would seem retaliatory. I came to the conclusion that the futility of trying to change this would only result in frustration, and so I left him to his reasonable devices. In short, I had become the thing I swore that I would not become, a government drone incapable of effecting change, content to sit there and watch the shit drip off the fan.

SB was becoming somewhat manageable, but still needed an occasional blocker to keep her from putting her foot in her mouth and pissing off customers and co-workers. She would often come storming into my office accusing someone or some agency of infringing on her territory. I usually only needed to break down the circumstances into small digestible pieces in order to convince her that the world was actually not out to get her. Not to mention that if she remained involved in all of the projects that she indicated belonged to her, she would have to be three people working twenty four hours a day in order to accomplish them all. Sometimes she got it, and sometimes she did not. I no longer cared. I had pulled her from EC's incompetence and put her on the projects that I considered important, e.g. the ones with the most visibility according to CZ. If she chose to spend her time worrying about what everyone else was doing, then that was her choice. I had given her the priorities and expected them to be completed. SB failed to understand that if you spend your days biting everyone's head off, at some point everyone is going to insist that you be euthanized.

SB spent her days biting the hand that fed her and then complained that no one wanted to work with her. Again, I had given up fighting this battle and spent my time running interference between her and coworkers and customers while directing her projects to conclusion.

GO was quick becoming a pain in my ass as well. GO's thinking was that he would manage any project of significance and then turn over the shit projects to me to complete. Any minor project, he also immediately dumped on my plate as if he were too good to deal with the crap day-to-day work. He quickly became quite annoyed as he realized that I wasn't going to just fold up and be his yes man cleaning up after him. My gut feeling is that CZ and GO were incapable of convincing EC to do his fucking job in a way that made them look good and decided to dump him on me to face the same issues. I am also aware that once he realized this fact, he began plotting a way to get rid of me by interfering in any project I attempted to bring to fruition simply by telling CZ that since he had not been involved, there was not consensus between all of the departments and that the project needed to be postponed. This was especially apparent in projects where I chose a different route than he would have taken and especially where I chose a vendor that was not one he was currently in bed with.

CZ, who had originally said that I would be in charge of managing the decisions of the engineers, would of course simply roll over and GO would simply kill the project.

As far as the staff goes, we were never sure who was in control, CZ or GO, but rumor was that it wasn't the person with the title of Director on her door. I won't tell you what the other rumors were, but the phrase "ewwww, gross" comes to mind.

The main problem that I had with GO was that his intentions were not clear, and in fact, seemed to be in direct conflict with the goals of the agency. You remember those goals don't you? To provide much needed services to the people of Minnesota? CZ had once informed me that the reason I was hired was to contribute in providing those services and that my twenty plus years of expertise would be a great asset to providing those services.

She did not explain that I would most likely never be allowed to provide those services, that I was simply a figurehead for the agency with no real power, and that all of my goals and objectives would be scrutinized and fed to me after being filtered by objectives that would eventually bear no resemblance to the original goals of the agency. She never explained that half of my department would still report directly to her and that the other half would be subject to the whims of the contractor she had hired – most likely due to the fact that a contractor would not jeopardize his sweet smelling position by daring to not agree with her particular neurosis.

That all of the managers and supervisors took issue with the fact that GO insisted on solutions that were directly against the desire and experience of the staff she had hired to manage ITS also seemed a bit odd. The bottom line is that a good manager isn't one who knows everything, but one that knows enough to know how little he or she knows and attempts to surround himself with people who can fill in the blanks. As we tried to fill in the blanks, GO usually insisted on solutions that were contrary and usually seemed to benefit him as opposed to the agency he was making an ass load of cash to support.

And so I ask you, my humble reader, the following question: If a contractor seems to be skirting the rules to the benefit of a particular vendor while ignoring the experience and desires of those who were hired to make those particular decisions for the department; and this particular contractor is given complete autonomy and the full endorsement of the department director who has no technical knowledge to make those decisions; and you were essentially told to mind your own fucking business when you began to question the whole arrangement, what would your inevitable conclusion be?

And so I struggled on, keeping in mind the little girl trapped in a Dutch attic while the Nazis paraded through the streets looking for her who once wrote: "I still believe that in spite of everything, that people are good." I wanted to believe that there were still good things to be accomplished at DHS and that not everyone there had completely given up and were only there for a paycheck and medical benefits.

At this point, I had already become incredibly disillusioned with the system, the people, and the policies. I began planning the outline for this book, knowing that at some point it would have to be written, and I spent many evenings wondering how long I would be able to sit in another meeting where nothing would be accomplished with people who contributed more to the failure of a project than to its success.

In the meanwhile, CZ, who at this point probably still believed that my experience and skills would be an asset to the agency, began farming me out as a technical representative to other agencies with the caveat that limited information was to be disseminated and that the content of any meeting which I attended was to be immediately transmitted to her.

I also continued to meet with other peer agencies in order to stem the tide of discontentment with the ITS department. I soon realized that it really didn't matter what the topic of conversation was, each agency was already knee deep in their dislike of ITS and were more than likely meeting only in order to meet the new guy and determine if there were any gaps into which they might wedge their own priorities.

At one point, I met with SR, who managed the child support enforcement division (CSED) and its peripheral staff. CZ had already warned me that SR did not like her at all (for some apparently unknown reason) and it was quite obvious that this was true as soon as I entered the room. Again, I had my suspicions as to why SR did not like her, but again decided to open with the benefit of doubt.

The history that I had been given was that CSED was notorious for implementing projects as pilots and then incorporating those "pilots" into their day-to-day operations to avoid the project charter process they found so mind-numbingly futile. During my meeting with SR, we did the now firmly established conversation dance around how our two agencies might work together going forward and how happy she was that I was there. SR informed me of some of the projects that they had been working on, and how they would like to further those projects by coordinating efforts between our two departments. One thing was very apparent in the course of this conversation. SR already knew the direction of her department's technology goals. She wasn't asking me if they could in fact go ahead with these projects, but was simply informing me of what they were going to do and making sure that I knew that unless we played ball, we would simply be left out of the mix. I have to say that sitting across the table from SR is akin to sitting across the table from an angry rhinoceros in a staring contest. SR is about 5 feet tall and I would guess at least two hundred and fifty to three hundred pounds of pure determination.

There are not many people who intimidate me given an equal set of circumstances, but to be quite honest about it, this woman scared the shit out of me. My mind kept drifting off as a televised flashback, only forward. I kept imagining SR reaching across the table and ripping my head off, or punching me in the face so hard it left my body. Whenever she came up with statements that began with phrases like "we would like" or "we are thinking about," my mind simply retreated to its safe zone and instructed my mouth to verbalize the only safe but non-committal statement I could think of. This statement was: "well, I don't see a problem with that, maybe we can work something out." I left the meeting feeling like I had just had the living shit kicked out of me, even if it had only been in my mind.

I also met with JS, who managed the purchasing and contracts for DHS and the wife of MS work worked for TS in the PMO. My relationship with JS started out amicably enough, and at one point I believed that at last there was someone who would listen to my concerns and guide me in the direction of addressing them appropriately. This was not the case. For one thing, over the past few months, I had worked with his wife on several projects and essentially considered her a control freak and a project management nightmare, but you will read more about that in the chapter outlining projects and their mismanagement. We talked for about an hour on how purchasing worked, contracts were negotiated and the whole of the DHS financial process.

Somewhere in our meeting, I felt comfortable enough to broach the subject that had I had been kicked in the teeth by CZ when I questioned how much we were paying for standard services, hardware, and software from vendors. When I mentioned that I had an uneasy feeling about some of the pricing and that I felt that specific vendors might be stacking the desk against other vendors with "perks" to some of our employees, he got up and closed the door. He returned to his desk indicating that he had some of the same suspicions and would like my help in ferreting out such illegal activities. He even went as far as to tell me that he would give me complete access to the ordering system known as EIOR so that I might report any suspicious activities to him directly. He also suggested that we use instant messaging over our blackberry devices to communicate, as it was the only messaging transport that could not be monitored by the state.

I thought that this was great, finally someone who actually cared about providing those services to the state and about ensuring that the rules were followed and that we as taxpayers got the best deal possible. I left that meeting feeling like it was going to be possible to get something accomplished, but that feeling was short lived. Over the next several months, I attended several vendor meetings with JS. He pretended that he was going to play hardball with a vendor and then caved. The contracts that were negotiated were no better than what I could negotiate with a vendor as a public citizen. I never actually received the full access to the EIOR system, so there was never any way for me to review the purchases made on behalf of ITS. Thus whatever shit he was concerned about kept flowing through the system with little or no oversight.

Inevitably, I decided that it all boiled down to this: DHS staff had already established favorite vendors, and contracts are subject to rules set forth by state purchasing agreements. Assuming that those purchasing agreements follow standard governmental procedures, bids are accepted and negotiated, but usually decided upon by one single factor – the lowest price, which is mandated by state rules. Vendors and distributors know this fact very well, as well as the fact that there are simply products that have no equal or would be too much of a pain in the ass to change, and thus they have less incentive to negotiate any lower pricing.

For example, ninety percent of state services ride on top of Microsoft operating systems and enterprise solutions. The truth of the matter is that UNIX or Linux, is almost always a cheaper alternative, performs as well as or better, and has substantially less hardware requirements. If you assume a thirty percent decrease in cost on hardware and an operating system at minimal or no cost, the state could save many, many millions of dollars on providing these services to the public. Which means…. Say it with me: "We could spend those millions of dollars on people who require healthcare or even, maybe, inspecting the odd bridge or two for potential failure points.

Yes, it would take some effort and some time to accomplish, but the inevitable solution would be more robust and cost effective, as well as the fact that the peripheral savings would also add up to millions of dollars in heating, air-conditioning, power use reduction, staffing, etc.

Microsoft knows that there is a substantial effort in converting these products and they also know that getting anything done at the state level takes ten times as long as it should and thus, Microsoft knows that the likelihood of them being walked out the door is close to zero. Now, you tell me what incentive Microsoft has to negotiate?

Before you all run out and call me a Microsoft hater, I qualify this by stating for the record that Microsoft make a pretty good product albeit at horribly inflated costs. I am not a Microsoft or Bill Gates hater in the slightest. The issue is providing a service to the taxpayers at the best cost and the state is not doing this, nor adequately attempting to do so, and everyone there knows it.

Another and more simple example is that about 4 months into my employment at DHS, I became incredibly annoyed at the speed of my desktop computer. I asked SB to order me some memory, and when she came back with the quote from the state approved vendor, it was almost four hundred dollars. I looked up the exact same memory on Amazon.com where it was listed at less than one hundred. I had to go to three people to get approval and wait 2 months to order it from Amazon and get more memory in my machine. I even offered to order and pay for it myself. CZ's response was "absolutely not, as this wasn't the way we did things at DHS."

The interesting thing in state government is that there is always some sort of initiative to improve processes, save money, and provide better and more efficient services to the public. The irony there is that state government is so irrevocably fucked, that every single initiative essentially ends up drowning in bureaucracy and political bullshit so that nothing ever happens with those initiatives. Still feel like your tax dollars are at work?

And so here we are several months into the position, and I find myself running into brick walls, landmines, and other structures that are designed to prevent one from actually accomplishing anything. Priorities are set at the whim of a tyrannical director, employees manipulate the system to benefit their own particular schedules, and every single day customers come to DHS with good ideas in search of solutions only to be met with promises that no-one will even attempt to keep.

As I had already decided to write about my experiences there, I found myself testing the system to locate its weaknesses, since there wasn't really any point in fighting against it any longer. GO was already spending much of his time there complaining to CZ that I wasn't engaged in the established processes. What he meant was that he was unhappy that I refused to roll over and give him full reign over my department. I was already having problems with my department, and he was only aggravating the situation.

For some odd reason, most of the employees were on a four-day week schedule, which means that they were either off on Friday or on Monday claiming that they worked ten-hour days. In order to find out how these ten hours days worked, I started coming in early to see what was going on. I found out that they did indeed come in at six in the morning. I also found out that they spent the first few hours of the morning bullshitting about anything non-work related and eating breakfast in the cafeteria in lieu of any actual DHS related work.

CZ was off every Monday claiming that she telecommutes. Since she did not have any sort of computer at home, I still wonder how the fuck the telecommute portion of this day off actually works. She did have a blackberry, however as you all know, since you cannot open documents or type any sort of lengthy response on any of those it makes it difficult to actually accomplish anything. This was also compounded by the fact that she was about as adept at using the thing as a monkey with six thumbs on each hand. She was constantly complaining that the server must have been malfunctioning due to the fact that she lost documents and contact information off the thing.

Many of us spent many hours trying to troubleshoot her particular issues knowing that the problem was that she was a fucking technical idiot, and not the hardware. In my ten years of using a PDA, I have never had information randomly appear or disappear unless I did something really stupid to cause it. I am really sorry, but if you are the only one out of thousands of people in the agency using the device, the problem isn't the device, it's you.

GO was only in the office two or three days per week, which also goes to my wondering exactly how the fuck much we were paying him. As I have mentioned before, you can't swing a dead cat without hitting a computer consultant. CZ assured me that he was at home working on DHS issues during the week, however when I called him, he was usually out running errands. Then at the beginning of or at the end of the day a barrage of emails would come through from him, I guess to prove that he was indeed working on DHS issues. We would usually not get answers until the following day when another barrage of emails would come through.

I would invite him to meetings to discuss the projects that I was working on, and he would decline the invitation without missing a heartbeat. Once the project was in the final stages, and we had made all of the decisions, he would show up and tell CZ that we did not have consensus between all of the relevant parties and so the project would be killed. This was especially apparent when the project had been designed using products or services that were not provided by his preferred vendors.

As I indicated, by this time I was only moments from saying to hell with it all or taking the route of complete complacency. After this had happened to five or six of my projects, I simple gave up fighting the system. I would take the projects that were assigned to me, find out what GO wanted, and then suggest that particular product or vendor. What then started to happen was that he would wait until all of the details were ironed out and then swoop in at the last minute informing CZ that because this project was so important and had irrevocable ties to other projects that he was working on, he should manage them. Of course, all of the irrelevant and downright shitty projects remained firmly on my plate.

CZ in the meanwhile had begun complaining that people had been complaining that I was not engaged in the processes. WTF? Of course I wasn't fucking engaged in the process, as there was no process to be engaged in. I had been tricked into babysitting two employees that she had basically allowed to bullshit their way into the sweet and savory position of almost never being able to be fired.

I had a contractor playing stupid games with the process and making an ass load of money doing so, and I had a director who seemingly picked priority projects randomly out of her ass and screamed at us when one of the customers had enough clout to complain to someone high enough on the DHS ladder that their very urgent project that they had let sit on their desk until the day before it was due wasn't getting enough attention from ITS.

Combine this with the fact that all of, and I do mean ALL of her direct reports considered her a fucking idiot, and spent their days whispering in corners about how fucked up she was while secretly hoping that she would die on the commute in to work one morning and you understand how impossible my position was.

The customers were another issue. In the unlikely event that a project was completed or a problem was solved for a customer, we would turn over the work to the customer for approval. Most of them would accept this project that was so urgent and then let it sit there for a few months while they went through their own kind of political bullshit. Several months later they would determine that something needed to be fixed or changed and then they would perform the infamous DHS email-forwarding trick.

The email trick worked this way. The customer, after being notified that the project was complete, would let the completed project sit there for months. Finally, they would begin to use or test the products that we had completed for them. They would find something that wasn't to their liking, decide that they need a change, or that the solution was old as an update had since been issued and needed to be installed. They would then send out an email stating that ITS fucked up, didn't complete the project, yada yada yada, when this could have all been resolved had they bothered to check the final product in the first place. To top it off, they would CC: everybody under the fucking sun with this invaluable new piece of information along with several snide remarks about how incompetent we were and how we fucked up their project causing them to be behind schedule.

This was particularly effective if their project received federal funding because they would almost always scream that the feds were about to pull the funding and that it was our entire fault. The complaint would slowly climb the ladder until "god" was pretty much involved and then CZ would get a phone call from someone with more pull than her, and we would all get our asses ripped for not completing the project when it was due three months ago. Of course this ass ripping usually concluded as most of her ass rippings did, with one of the following statements:

"Johanna is so angry right now I can't believe it"

or

"you have embarrassed the agency once again",

or

"I still haven't been able to get the dock in my back yard off the lake, but this guy keeps saying that he will come by and do it, but he hasn't shown up yet and I'm getting worried"

This is how things work at ITS. Nothing gets accomplished unless it's an edict from the commissioner, it's never anyone in upper management who takes the bullet, and you end up feeling like shit at the end of most meetings because first and foremost, shit rolls downhill.

And so my humble readers, by this time you have probably figured out that I had just about given up believing in fighting the good fight, and I apologize for this. But how long can one keep beating his head against a brick wall before he passes out? The way I saw my job was that it was to make my boss look good, but not to continually cover up her incompetence and paranoia; and to provide services to the people of Minnesota as efficiently and expeditiously as possible and at the least possible cost, but not to spend ninety percent of my time fucking around in meetings that went no where with people who's only purpose was self serving administrative bullshit.

So yes, I apologize for throwing in the towel, but even though my sense of self was still in tact, the mighty machine called bureaucracy had crushed my spirit. DHS doesn't do projects because they need to be done. DHS does projects that will raise the stature of an individual, individuals, or department; or proves the absolute necessity of those individuals or department; or because someone higher up the ladder has enough clout or simply screams loud enough to get it done.

Budgeting is a fucking joke as well. Because people spend most of their days not getting anything accomplished, April and May sees a fury of activity for everyone to spend as much money as possible since anything that wasn't spent during the previous budgeting cycle gets dumped back in the general fund.

What happens is that during the last few months, every agency under the sun crawls out from every rock in Minnesota with projects that absolutely, must be done in the next twenty minutes or so. Never mind that the specs for this project have been sitting on some idiot's desk for the last 11 months. For some reason this previously unheard of project must be done now, and according to them the sun will probably fall out of the sky if it is not. I think we have covered a small amount of the project charter process and the so-called projects management office, but more on that later. Obviously ITS – being horribly behind in the projects they already have on their plate – is obliged to receive and review these projects one at a time, where they are promptly put on the list of projects, or as DHS likes to call them, the "shit we ain't gonna do and who the fuck do they think they are anyway?" list. There will be more on that particular nightmare later, but let's get back to and conclude our chapter on the people and personalities of DHS.

By now I think most people had figured out that my level of contentment was in the toilet. Perhaps it was the fact that I spent most of my time in my office only dealing with things as they came up; managing projects and situations from a distance; and that I had also begun simply agreeing with my peers on all of the ideas that they came up with. It made no sense to suggest new ideas or technologies. DHS was firmly rooted in its failed policies and procedures and wasn't going to be dislodged from them at any time soon.

Trying to get actual answers from people was like pulling teeth, and my director was absolutely hopeless in this matter. To ask a question about priorities to CZ was akin to asking an elephant if they were truly afraid of mice.

The question would be ignored and more than likely your ass would be trampled on. The answer to that question by the way was twofold: that the executive team decided the priority of projects and that all of the projects that came from the executive team were our number one priority. I knew, as did everyone else that this was not only untrue but also impossible. How the fuck can you have multiple number one priorities, much less fifty of them?

CZ and I met weekly on Friday mornings and week after week I simply imagined myself standing up, reaching across the table to grab her by the shirt collar and pulling her forward where I would scream into her face the following words:

> *"THERE CAN'T BE FIFTY FUCKIN NUMBER ONE PRIORITIES YOU STUPID BITCH, NOW LOOK AT THE*

LIST IN FRONT OF YOU AND GIVE ME THE TOP THREE THINGS TO WORK ON".

Fantasies aside, this sort of behavior would more than likely be frowned upon and would probably result in my immediate involvement with a pair of handcuffs, denial of unemployment benefits, and a restraining order or two. Of course, now that I think about it, it might have been worth it. Everyone else already thought she was nuts and an extremely loud and very public "fuck you" might have cheered up everyone who worked for her for once.

SB had more than likely figured out this methodology and adopted it as her own as she seemed to retreat to the security of her cubicle most of the time. My relationship with EC had also mellowed and he and I met once a week to discuss everything that was going on in the department. This usually centered on him handing me a very confusing set of purchasing EIORs for approval and I pretty much just said to hell with it and signed them.

GO avoided me unless our two areas intersected in some odd way, and I usually just agreed with whatever the hell he wanted in order to not have him running to mommy CZ complaining that I wasn't engaged. I am pretty sure that he recognized this as the proverbial "fuck you asshole" that it was and continued to whine to CZ whenever possible that my lips were not pressed as firmly to his ass as he would have liked them.

SB resigned sometime in the next few weeks. I had been expecting it and was a bit disappointed in the fact that she had let them beat her. She had accepted another position, and I pulled her aside to congratulate her and give her the required speech of I am happy for you, or you deserve better than this place, or it's all for the best, and on and on. I knew she was angry, and she did try to hide it from me, but tears tend to give shit like that away. Besides you don't give a place that many years of your life and just walk out with no feelings whatsoever.

And whether or not she believed me, I meant all of the things I said. I had grown fond of her and truly believed that she was trying to do an impossible job in a sea of assholes that fought her every inch of the way. Good Luck, SB.

The week in September, which was supposed to be the end of my probationary period at DHS, was also the beginning of the end. At our weekly meeting, CZ informed me that she had been receiving complaints about my level of engagement. I am pretty sure that she was mostly eluding to the fact that Bacon Boy, as I had appropriately renamed GO, had decided that I was a detriment to his continued cushy career at DHS; and to the fact that I had responded to an email request from the legal department in direct opposition to something CZ had told them. I guess I had violated the golden rule of not pissing off your boss by disagreeing with her a few months before your probation is over. Deep down I already knew that I was fucked, so why not go out in a blaze of glory.

We had received an email from legal (printed in the back of this book), outlining a data request from Minnesota Public Radio concerning the recent SCHIP bill that that asshole in Washington had recently VETOED. The email essentially asked if we could retrieve any emails having to do with SCHIP from mailboxes mostly belonging to DHS commissioners, assistant commissioners and other official or legal entities in the department.

CZ had told them that the maximum that we could go back was thirty days and that any searches on the ITS side would be practically impossible so they would have to do this from inside the commissioners mailbox. Keeping in mind that I pretty much no longer gave a happy rat's ass what she said, and the fact that I was tired of lying to other agencies to cover her ass, I responded differently.

I responded with the fact that, yes we could of course search for these emails in all of these boxes on the back end and that if they would kindly provide me with the key words they wanted us to search on, I would provide them with the results almost immediately.

CZ stopped me in the hallway and ripped me a new one. If you could see my ass right now, I am pretty sure that there are still teeth marks in it. The most astounding thing is that she wasn't so much upset that we could locate the data, but that I had contradicted her in an email that others higher up the food chain would see, thus making her appear like the uninformed liar she was.

She informed me that she was too busy to talk about it now, but that I should add it to my list and we would talk about it tomorrow at our weekly meeting. This was the meeting where she informed me that she had been receiving complaints about my level of engagement. Of course, she wouldn't tell me who any of the people were that were lodging these complaints, the same way she wouldn't tell me who seemed so shocked that a black man spoke English and could put a few sentences together.

I am going to pause here for a moment and direct the following three words to whoever that individual happened to be. "FUCK YOU, ASSHOLE."

Anyway, CZ then informed me that she was dissatisfied with my progress and that as was her right under union guidelines, she was extending my probation another three months. She repeated all of the standard lines, asking me if I were happy there, if there was another position I could see myself doing, yada, yada, yada, and I said nothing.

She asked me if I had any questions, yada yada, did I understand what she was saying, yada, yada, yada, and I said nothing.

I couldn't believe that she having this conversation with me as if we were best friends. She was smiling and laughing, and the deepest hope in my mind was that she was sitting there wondering if I were going to rip her throat out. Nope, this was not my style as the concept for the book was well under way, and I felt that I had more than enough information to nail her tits to the wall. I also already knew then what I am sure that she was hoping that I didn't know which was that she had already made up her mind, but was simply going through the motions so that she could say that I was warned.

She didn't seem to remember that we had walked through the bullshit of what you could and could not do to a union employee in terms of disciplinary actions. The golden rule is that you don't bullshit a bullshitter and you don't bullshit one that you have previously explained your particular kind of bullshit to. I left her office and slowly began to remove my personal items from there a little bit at a time at the end of each day.

I continued to "be" there – attending the meetings that I was invited to and simply agreeing with the majority of the table on whatever the topic of conversation happened to be. We replaced SB with someone from operations, and life went on. I joined teams to help determine the best way to coordinate projects when we were allowed to actually work on them. I continued my weekly meetings with CZ and informed her of what I was working on and of the progress of it. She sat across the table from me with that stupid grin of hers pretending that everything was wonderful and going well. This was more than likely due to the fact that she had finally gotten that fucking dock out of the lake rather than any sort of admiration she was feeling towards my department and me.

When SB had resigned, CZ was abso-fucking-lutely elated, although of course she couldn't show that to me, but you could tell by the fact that the ends of her mouth kept trying to shoot skywards every time SB's name was mentioned. I will say that I admire her restraint, as I am sure that it took the strength of Hercules to not fall off her chair with the joy of knowing that she had won that particular battle and fucked over another individual under her oppressive system of management.

In the next few weeks, I also made no secret of the fact that she had extended my probation. In fact, I told everyone I could that she had done so and that my time there was limited. It's funny how people get nicer to each other when something bad happens to them. People suddenly wanted to hear my opinion about things that were going on and often iterated the well known fact that our director was generally thought of as an incompetent dingbat and that I shouldn't worry about it because if she actually wanted me gone, she would have done so already.

Apparently they had not been paying as close attention as I had previously thought. CZ's number one reason for having survived for so long at DHS is her ability to cover her own ass above all else. Firing me outright would give rise to rumors and speculations. Extending my probation and then terminating me at the end of it would show everyone that she had covered the bases and could in fact say that she had given me every opportunity to earn my keep, so to speak. Never mind the previous ten months where managerial instruction was pretty much non-existent and my sole guidance from her had been on ways to keep all of the ITS skeletons in the closet. She was on a roll having gotten rid of SB, and now I was next.

About a month before this extension was to expire, CZ pulled me off the remainder of my projects sighting the wishes of the other agencies. Keep in mind that these were the same agencies that more than likely would have kissed my ass on national television eleven months ago. These were the same agencies that eleven months ago, were stopping into my office to tell me how wonderful it was to have someone there who actually gave a fuck and would try to get their projects pushed through the bullshit system. And now apparently, these same agencies that had previously extolled the virtues of my stinkless shit were somehow of the opinion that I was not being responsive to their needs.

I wonder how that happened? I guess bacon boy had finally managed to drive home the final nail, and so I decided to completely hang her ass out to dry. Told her that I really wanted my job and then I asked her if I had time to fix this. That fake smile of hers disappeared faster than shit through a goose. What she said was, “I don’t know Vincent.” What she meant was, “dear boy, you are so fucking fucked already that I can hardly stand it.” I kept removing my things from my office knowing that I had made her uncomfortable. It was a good feeling.

CZ would have had to process the paper work no later than my one-year anniversary on December thirteenth. To wait any longer she would have had to actually do some work in the weeks before Christmas. My last and final meeting with her was on the sixth of December at nine in the morning. I knew this was the day, expected that this was the day, and the upside down piece of paper on the table when I walked in for our meeting confirmed that this was the day. I closed my notebook and waited. She informed me that we only had one thing to talk about and that was the fact that she had run out of time on my extension.

Her final quote was that we could call it philosophical differences, but that it simply wasn't working out. She went through all of the canned bullshit explanations about how I would receive information from HR regarding benefits and that I had the right to meet with her again, with or without a union rep, yada, yada, yada. The only thing I kept thinking was that I wished she would shut the fuck up, and that I was glad that she had gotten that damned dock out of the lake because if she had brought that up again, I would have strangled her right then and there.

She also asked if I wanted some time and that I could come back to get my things. There was no way in hell that I was going to come back there in the middle of the night like I had done something wrong. I told her that I did not want a meeting with her and that I would take my things with me right then and there and then I returned to my office to gather the remainder of my things.

I turned in my ID and blackberry and walked out with a bag, a box and my pride. I had not fallen prey to the bullshit that was DHS ITS. I had not become a fucking government drone only out to collect a paycheck and benefits. I had tried to accomplish the things that were important to me, and provide the services that were important to the State of Minnesota. In short, I had tried to do the job that I believed I had been hired to do and I drove home feeling a little shitty, and a lot relieved that it was finally over.

In closing this chapter, it reminds me of many things that could probably be added to it to provide additional examples and as I go back though the editing process I am sure that some of it will look substantially different than it does at this point. Through the magic of editing, I am sure that you will not know what those things are, but the basics stem from the fact that it is not my intention to shame or embarrass the many people at the sate who are there to do the best job they can.

The more naïve of those who are not there for that reason will more than likely assume that I wrote this book for those reasons alone. They can believe what they will, and yes I have managed to take a few pot-shots at certain people here and on the website as well, but not doing so would have been so out of character that it simply had to be done. Perhaps some of those people are still at DHS and if this is the case, I hope that they will take a good look at their position and ask themselves why?

The people like SB & EC who have played a large part of this chapter are important as well. It's important for me to say that I thoroughly enjoyed working with them and that I do not believe that they have failed the system, but that the system has failed them. Most employers ask their employees to run marathons for them, and most employees are happy do so. However, most employers don't tie your shoelaces together and then hand you a fucking bowling ball at the last minute to carry with you.

My mistake was in believing that I could change the system and maybe even some of the people. Information Technology is not difficult, people are. Most people want simple things and they want them to be easy. They want to be able to call a number to get information and have that information be the correct information.

Single mothers want to be able to sit across from someone down at the MinnesotaCare offices and explain to someone how their asshole husband whom they put through law school left them with three children and without any money for some bimbo the day after he graduated, and to have that person walk them through the process of getting healthcare instead of guiding them into an endless loop of bullshit and paperwork only to be finally declined because once upon a time they made too much money.

But most of all, I think that most people when given a job and an acceptable way of doing that job, will be more than happy to do their best at it. DHS didn't provide that acceptable way, for me at least, and I am truly sorry for those in the same situations who wish to change the system, but who are still stuck in that hopeless loop of bureaucracy and bullshit.

I will close this chapter by simply saying that in many ways I am truly relieved to have escaped with my sense of self intact and to no longer be under the thumb of those who have decided to manipulate the system instead of working to change it.

CHAPTER 3

PROJECT NON-MANAGEMENT:

Projects at DHS typically come from one of several sources: an agency need, a customer of the agency, a legislative mandate, or a federal mandate. There may be others, but for the sake of brevity let's stick to those four.

Over the course of my year there, we at DHS had spent several thousand man-hours attempting to define solid processes and procedures that could be utilized to enforce the rules of managing a project. Because the scope of projects at DHS tend to be quite large, many agencies and individuals are involved in making a project happen and specific considerations for those projects must all be taken into account.

Customer and agency needs are easy, as the growth of technology over the last few years has mandated that certain solutions are not only desirable, but also required in the normal course of business. A few of the basic ones are technologies such as informational websites, email, document storage, telephones, etc. These types of enterprise solutions are a dime a dozen and in general, easily accomplished and distributed throughout any organization. They perform basic functions that are easily utilized by those in the organization.

Solutions mandated by our local legislators or federal agencies tend to be a bit more complex and usually require a higher level of technical knowledge due to the absolute requirements each law tends to provide for. For example, putting in a stop sign is a very easy solution to control traffic on a residential street, however putting in stoplights at a four way boulevard intersection requires specialized knowledge and expertise. In order to accomplish the latter, you are beginning to get into traffic patterns, seasonal changes, time changes, and all sorts of details that your original stop sign would not take care of and without which it would never serve to keep traffic from becoming a complete cluster fuck during rush hour.

The complexity of these technology solutions is also compounded by several facts which I will now outline for you, but the easiest way of putting it is that people are generally pretty fucking stupid when you get right down to it. You would be amazed at some of the support calls I have fielded over the years only to find out that the user on the other end was bitching and pissing at me about something they did to fuck up their machine and did not want to admit it. A second and equally simple explanation is that given half a chance, most people will fuck you over without thinking twice about it. I will give you an example of each and why these two things contribute to the rising cost of technology as a whole.

A few years back, a sales guy I will refer to as Bob, called into the office to report that he could not dial into the office to connect to the network. As the more observant of you have already surmised, I said that this was a sales person, and even the worst fucking asshole sales person in the world thinks that everything is about him and of course since he could not get into the network he was of course about loose a gazillion dollar sale and it was all due to the fact that he could not get into his email.

Two of my technical support people spent about an hour on the phone receiving verbal abuse that ran the gamut from how completely useless and idiotic we were to which orifice our mothers happened to have spat us out from while she resided in the bowels of hell. The issue was that he simply could not connect to our network and therefore something must be wrong with our network. We spent several hours running diagnostics and other tests, dialing in with our own laptops, etc, only to discover what we already knew which was that he had fucked something up and was looking for someone to blame. Eventually he just hung up on us after very loudly screaming a few fucks and assholes, and something about calling my boss and, I think complementing my mother on her extremely large ass and so we went back to doing whatever it was we were doing before that idiot called in.

About two hours later, he called back with a question and my guys refused to take the call having had quite enough of his abuse, so they passed the call to me which, as manager, I was obliged to take. He had obviously calmed down quite a bit and made no mention of his previous problem, and so you know that I had to ask if he were now able to dial in.

Me: Hey Bob, did you get your problem solved… eh, you know, was it like an issue with your local telephone company or something?

Bob: Oh, yeah… (He paused for a really long fucking time) uh... well, I was like plugged into my daughters phone line instead of the office one. My daughters phone line has long distance blocked so it wouldn't let me dial into Minneapolis from Florida. (This followed by another really long pause.)

OK, I really, really didn't want to let this asshole off the hook, but since I had him on speaker phone and all of the people he had previously suggested were mindless douche bags were listening in, and were pretty much on the floor laughing their asses off and I was pretty sure he would hear them trying to hold back the laughter, I decided to not pursue it any more and so I just let it drop.

Me: So bob, that's good, I'm glad it worked out. So what's your other question?

By now my sides hurt from the laughter, and it was all I could do to talk while gesturing for everyone who couldn't keep it quiet to get out.

Bob: So yeah, like I was saying, I got dialed in and logged into email, but I don't have any.

Me: what do you mean you don't have any?

Bob: None, I have not received an email in about a week.

I knew this was impossible because all sales people were sent sales briefs daily. He should have at least seven of them, plus that big okey dokey on the gazillion dollar sale he was expecting, and so I turned around and logged into the server and then into his email account where I discovered that he had about sixty unread emails. Again, the problem was somewhere on his end.

I informed him of his current email status and walked him through the ten or so things that stupid people usually do on their computers when they can't find something. I made sure that he was in fact dialed in, logged into his account, authenticated on the domain, yada, yada, yada… and still nothing.

After about an hour I gave up and offered to overnight him a new laptop if he would send me his and he agreed. I told him how to send it in and then hung up the phone. I sat there staring at the screen trying to figure out what the fuck he could have done to the computer when it hit me like a twenty-ton brick. I called Bob back and asked him to dial into the network again and open outlook. He did this and when he had outlook on the screen I asked him to look across the top of the program to find the column header labeled “date.” When he indicated that he had found it, I told him to click on it.

By the sound of the happy euphoria on the other end of the phone, it was quite obvious that his email had now re-sorted itself to show the newest emails on top instead of the bottom, and I was again waving a hysterical crowd of support engineers out of my office.

Bob quickly issued his thanks, not for not pointing out his particularly high level of stupidity, but for fixing whatever was wrong on the network. I accepted his apology, and hung up the phone, as I could no longer hold in the laughter. Like I said, when it comes down to it, most people are pretty fucking stupid.

The second series of examples that contributes to the rising cost of technology I will give you are some things that you are all quite familiar with – SPAM and Viruses, coupled with identity theft.

Everyone considers spam a nuisance, but what most people do not bother to think about is that SPAM is not only a pain in the ass, it also costs YOU money to receive it. Junk mail sent via the USPS is a pain in the ass, but it costs the sender money to send it and so this is quickly becoming a seldom-used method of advertising. On the other hand, sending out a few hundred million SPAM messages costs the sender absolutely nothing. In addition to the Internet connection you pay for to receive it, it also costs you the time and energy it takes to sort through all of the shit in your inbox to find the emails you actually want. Then you may have even invested in software to filter out the spam, which is an additional expense.

Consider the cost of those things along with the Anti-virus software you paid for, the shredder you bought because some asshole might go through your trash and find your credit card receipts, the credit monitoring service you now pay for, and the stress and paranoia we all experience every time we pay a bill or order the latest this or that on the internet. All of these threats are very real and a complete pain in the ass, but they are all something we put up with because we are too lazy to drag our fat asses out to the local Target and why should we when EBay or Amazon.com will deliver it to our door by eight A.M. the very next morning. Yes, I am calling you all lazy, fat slugs and yes, I am including myself in that category at the same time.

The ugly little secret about SPAM is that it works. If some lazy fucking asshole sitting in his basement office in the middle of the night presses the send key on his computer, a few hundred million emails whips out to the internet by the time he wakes up in the morning.

If he is hawking some stupid item for only $5.99, and one thousand people respond, that asshole has just made about $6000 for doing nothing more than pressing a button. If he does this only 3 nights per week, that asshole makes about six million dollars per year for doing nothing more than wasting your time and he does it all with the press of a single button. The sad thing is that he may not even have a product, or is selling information only. The other dirty little secret about SPAM is that most people are truly disappointed with what they might actually receive, if they receive anything at all. I am not going to lecture you about responding to SPAM emails, except to say that you should ignore them because your chances of getting ripped off are pretty high. As an IT professional, if I had my way, I would catch those fuckers and execute them on Friday night pay-per-view. Now that would be worth the $5.99.

Anyway, those are two examples of why technology starts to get complicated and why the costs of it keep skyrocketing. The stupid people and the scumbags who are too lazy to go out and get a fucking job cost you time, energy and money and those simplistic technology solutions that I mentioned at the beginning of this chapter are now becoming your traffic lights at the four way intersection. If there is a way to exploit technology, there are always people out there who will figure out a way to do it and to be quite frank, there is little we can do to stop it.

When I taught computer technology at a school in Minneapolis, I would to send my students to porn sites in order to explain certain aspects of technology. You may think the websites that you visit are all pretty now with rotating images and video on demand because the technology fell out of some geeks ass during a wet dream, when the truth is more simplistic than that. The reason images and video expanded so rapidly in the web was because the porn industry needed a faster way to distribute their products. Most of that technology started in the porn industry and was simply expanded on by the rest of us.

It was also important that I explain the basics of soft skills to students would face the challenges of dealing with people who don't have any knowledge of technology but are required to utilize it on a daily basis. People simply expect that when they press the send button on an email that they have painstakingly composed, that email will do whatever it does to get where it is being sent and arrive there as intended and without any difficulties. When it does not, these people have no patience for the reasons it did not arrive, but simply want to have the problem fixed as of yesterday.

I was once standing at the Minneapolis St. Paul airport waiting to catch a seriously delayed flight to London. The woman in front of me, along with her daughter, spent no less that fifteen minutes screaming at the guy behind the counter that come hell or high water that they needed to be on that plane. I think that had they not crossed the line and become abusive, he might have indeed found an alternate route for them to complete their trip. Once they had implied that he was incompetent and the threats began, all bets were pretty much off and I and everyone else in line knew that the only way this woman was going to get to London was to begin walking. I also knew this because once I arrived at the counter and graciously asked if there was anything he could do for me, it only took about thirty seconds for him to find me a seat on the flight. While I understood this woman's high level of frustration, I don't understand why she didn't' realize that the two feet of snow on the ground hadn't personably been arranged for by the guy behind the ticketing counter. Even if it had been, the successful completion of her trip was completely at his discretion. We, as a whole, are a consumerist and impatient society and the fact that we can order a pizza in thirty minutes or less doesn't mean that we always need a pizza in thirty minutes or less.

I bring these things up for two reasons. First of all, they give you an idea of what it takes to run a safe and secure technology environment comprised of several thousand impatient people and complicated technology solutions. Secure websites, firewalls and password authentication, secure financial institutions, fingerprint readers, and the like all exist for the same reason you have a lock on your house, and that is to keep the assholes from stealing your shit when you are not looking.

So in a very short period of time we have gone from a simplistic set of technology tools all run by some post-pubescent, pimply-faced nerd geek boy in the back room to a very specialized set of skills run by talented people with years of experience and specialized knowledge and training.

The second reason is to have explained why technology has become to complex to the average user and to explain what it takes to protect us all from ourselves. Of all of the millions of people reading this book, (I hope) I would guess that one out of every ten of you have a virus or worm on your computer that you don't know about, and that less than one out of every three people reading this book has backed up the data on your computer in the last year. And exactly how fucking stupid is that? All of your family photos, financial data, diagrams, emails, and other things you deemed important enough to store on your computer are either open for some asshole you don't know to access or subject to loss because you are too fucking lazy to drop a CD in once a month to back up your data. Oh, well, such is life and there are quite a few companies out there willing to take several thousand of your hard earned dollars to recover your data when your hard drive crashes, so what the hell, don't worry about it. Anyway, back to the projects process at DHS.

This chapter is written mostly for the customers at DHS and will serve to explain why you have such a hard time getting ITS to do anything. The rest of you will find this interesting because in explaining to the customers why they aren't getting any decent services from ITS, you will understand why your tax dollars slip quietly into the black hole known as DHS ITS.

Projects at DHS usually begin when a customer comes to ITS with an idea or a requirement, or a mandate or some other thing that is needed for whatever reason. These are divided into two distinct areas with one of them being standard services and the other being an actual project. A standard service is something that IT provides on a regular basis, like adding a new employee to the network, or resetting a password, or setting up or fixing a desktop. Requests like these are pretty easy and usually do not take too long. Standard services are usually routed through the helpdesk where they are assigned to an engineer or to operations to complete. Even the more complex standardized services can usually be handled with a minimum of fuss. Although, DHS has several ingenious ways of fucking those up as well, so take notice as to how you present your request.

Take for example a firewall change. A firewall change is something one of the security experts do to route information from one place to another while making sure that that data cannot be compromised by anyone who is not authorized to see that data. I am not going to go into the complexities of how the network is configured, as I am sure that the DHS legal department would have a field day kicking my ass for letting all of that out, but suffice to say that there is a lot of money and effort spent on keeping things secure at DHS – which is a very good thing for all concerned.

For the sake of simplicity, let's say that SOS (State Operated Services) designs a new database at their main facility that keeps track of all of the patients admitted to another facility in another part of the state. It's easier and more cost effective to keep that database located at the main facility and simply allow the staff that inputs the data at the other location to access the database remotely. The reason it is more cost effective is because all of the people who work on the database are located at the main facility, as well as the fact that the database needs to be backed up and monitored and moving all of that data from point B to point A can be very expensive and time consuming. It would be like you trying to download all of the information from Google to your own computer. Even on the fastest line, it would be almost impossible for you to successfully store or manage the data, so it's just easiest to keep it there and access it remotely.

So, now that SOS has this new really cool database, they want it to be accessible to the staff at the other location and of course the easiest thing would be to put up a website on the Internet, but let's not forget about the lazy scumbags out there. Personal and governmental data is a valuable commodity, as well as the fact that Uncle Sam requires this information to be kept private and on a need to know basis. The minute that database showed up on the internet, every scumbag data collector would be out there beating on it twenty four hours per day until they got in, and eventually really they would get in, as some of these people are very talented hackers.

So the way to connect these two sites is to still use the Internet, but to create a private way for the information to travel back and forth. This methodology utilizes what we will call for the sake of brevity an encrypted tunnel. Suppose your teenage daughter was secretly playing tonsil hockey or worse with the neighbor boy after you explicitly forbid her to do so. Both she and he know that if they simply go outside and enter the others house, the nosy fucker across the street would see them and get on the phone informing you of their violating the rules.

So instead, she goes down into the basement, slips behind the water heater where she knows you will never go because you are afraid of spiders, and digs straight down and then over to the neighbors house where she emerges through the hole that punk started at the same time she started hers which is hidden by his fathers secret three hundred volume autographed magazine stash of "chicks with dicks." Now that they have their secret tunnel their forbidden tryst goes on and you and his perverted father are none the wiser. That is a quite fine example of an encrypted tunnel and you can thank me later for the giggles.

To create this tunnel, a secret route is created between the Internet firewall on the SOS side and the firewall on the DHS side and finally the firewall at the remote location. This routing information tells the data from the database to go to the network at the remote location and nowhere else. And because it is encrypted with all sorts of complicated hash marks and secret codes, it also has the net effect of telling anyone who tries to access the data while it travels to and from the remote location to fuck off.

These types of standard services are usually pretty simple and subject only to a request, a quick review by the security team and about a half hour for one of the security experts to perform the creation of the tunnel. Occasionally, these sorts of standardized requests get quite a bit more complicated, but you get the idea.

Where it gets really complicated is when a standard service enters the project arena, which requires ten tons of investigation, design, some serious financial backing and even more bullshit, departmental posturing and thirty five people who have pretty much already decided that you ain't getting what you are going to ask for.

To start at the beginning, and eliminate the easy ones, I will simply explain it this way. If something comes down from the legislators such as a change in the law, which requires that information be changed or updated, or something comes down from the feds requiring that you keep track of how many homeless people are urinated on, beaten and thrown in the trunk of a squad car, then you are pretty much set to have your project completed. Go home and have a cold one. A project sent to ITS in this way is akin to an eleven foot tall, six hundred pound giant showing up at your door with a very imposing club slung over his shoulder requesting oral sex. You might not want to do it, and depending on your particular orientation you might actually be severely grossed out at the thought of going down on Quasimodo's ugly older brother.

But the truth of the matter is that more than likely, you are going to end the conversation you were having with your grandmother on the phone, run off to locate your kneepads, a towel, and a bottle of Listerine and set about the task of orally getting this guy off.

These are the types of projects that are never, ever questioned by anyone, and usually are received at ITS by someone more important than you sending out an email with vague details about the project, who ordered it, and how quickly you are going to drop whatever the fuck you are currently working on to get it done. Unfortunately, these projects show up about three or four times a month and are almost immediately added to the list of the other number one priority projects that are more important than any of the other number one projects. In other words, your pile of shit just got bigger and stinkier and there won't be a single sheet of toilet paper for miles around.

The other kind of project that we can eliminate are the projects that are internal to ITS. These projects are usually associated with the services that ITS can provide, but are not directly reliant on them. An example of this would be that the ITS department manages the disk space that the rest of the agencies use to store their data. When this disk space gets low, ITS must order and install more drives to accommodate the shortage in space. This isn't really a big deal, but in order to replace drives, data must be backed up or moved while the new drives are installed and then restored. So these projects will obviously get done, because if they weren't PF wouldn't be able to store those eighty or ninety thousand emails that he keeps in his inbox. (NO I AM NOT KIDDING!)

So I will say to the important people who happen to have the fortunate position of managing those kinds of projects, good for you, or as my good friend at DHS, WD would say: "Rock On."

The second kind of projects are those that come from within the agencies themselves. While the agencies may be tasked with some sort of federal or legislative mandate, these projects are usually less important as their mandates usually specify what is to be accomplished, but not exactly how to accomplish it. As long as these agencies provide the required services, their funding is continued and everyone gets to keep their jobs. One of the more troubling agencies in this respect is SSIS.

SSIS is in charge of all of the data that all of the counties in Minnesota keep on child welfare cases. According to the management at SSIS, they might as well be pretty much in charge of keeping track of every pimple on every ass of every child in the state of Minnesota. These guys play the "we are pretty much godlike" card every chance they get, and I am pretty sure that I heard the "we are federally mandated to take care of the children of Minnesota" line about two hundred times before I was there even a month.

Don't get me wrong, these guys really are doing a good thing, but WT reminds me of Rudy Giuliani over the past five years. Jesus, you would think that guy fucking rebuilt New York City with his own two hands. The problem with SSIS is that they play that card just way too much, and it usually seems to be used so that they can abuse the system. All that usually does is just piss people off, and as you all know, you don't bite the hand that feeds you unless you already have a firm grip on the balls of whomever happens to own that hand. They don't, and most of their requests get batted down by CZ somewhere between breakfast and a very long, overly complicated story about the rosebush outside her window that mysteriously died.

The problem with these agencies having a specific mandate, but relatively few guidelines as to how to fulfill it, is that they tend to be so far down the totem pole that, as far as ITS is concerned, most of their projects will fall somewhere below the other federally mandated projects and that lump of shit you skipped over on your way to work this morning. So an agency tasked with tracking infant deaths in Minnesota, who up until now were using an abacus and a jar of jellybeans to keep track of these numbers is pretty much shit out of luck when they go to request something more substantial. Uncle Sam really doesn't give a damned how they keep track of the data, only that they do so.

I use that particular project because as a parent, it really pissed me off when everyone in ITS pretty much wasted their time asking questions about the project, and as soon as they walked out of the door flipped them the proverbial finger, but more on that later.

As I was starting to say, these projects are routed to ITS and delivered to the door of the Business Relationship Team. The first contact portion of a project charter is usually handled by AH, a state contractor who was originally hired to do something else. I forget what, and it was probably something I never really understood anyway. That's the problem when you try to manage an empire built on sand. You tend to loose a lot of shit when you aren't looking, and all you have to show for it when you get home is a rash between the cheeks.

AH takes all of the initial information and creates a document called the project charter. You might at this point want to go back and review the section where I described what a conversation with him is like. AH is by no means a stupid individual, but rather he is in my humble opinion one of those people who adds complication to simple things. Given his position as a contractor, I do not begrudge him this at all. If you will remember my earlier statement about people, I now amend the "people will fuck you over given half a chance" statement to include "and will take advantage of any convenient situation that allows it."

The project charter document is distributed to the department managers and supervisors for review, and every other Tuesday or so the representatives from the department making the request are invited to a meeting to discuss the details of the project. At the project charter meeting, all of the ITS managers and supervisors sit around the table with them and ask questions to determine what resources would be required to complete the task. Keeping in mind that most of these people are not technical, do not wish to be technical, and simply are attempting to receive a service from ITS which they require and deserve, we sometimes we were required to dig deep and pull the required information out of these people forcibly.

In the case of the agency tasked with keeping track of infant deaths in the state of Minnesota, they wanted a database that could be used to track this data as well as a web server to provide access to this data. They also wanted this database to be able to import and export data from the federal government system that kept track of the national infant death data so that the two data sources could be compared.

A system like this would require a simple server to house the software and an engineer or two to install and configure the server and software. It would also require a review by security to ensure that not only was the data as safe as possible, but that the other systems from the feds would be unable to compromise the newly implemented DHS system.

The really cool thing was that they had already researched and decided on the tool that they wanted to use, and all we had to do was install the damned thing for them and provide access to them. As I sat there, I was guessing that the implementation of this system would probably take less than a few hours to implement once the server and software had arrived. AH thanked them for meeting with us and told them that we would get back to them.

After they had left, the very first things said were something akin to the following:

"This is so far down the food chain that it will never be done".

"There is no way in hell that this will ever be done. CZ won't even look at this"

And AH added the following:

"Yeah, so I'll just put this on the list and we can get back to them later."

Still being pretty new, I jumped in and asked the following question.

"Why not, this is pretty easy and should take only a few hours."

Of course a barrage of answers then hammered me, including the fact that I was new and didn't understand how things worked; That CZ would never even bother to listen to this project, yada, yada, yada....

And so I shut up, but not without speaking to the fact that we should be able to do it, and that everyone around that table was a parent and why wouldn't we want to do it? And I was firmly and resignedly ignored. I kept my mouth shut for the rest of the meeting.

I went to CZ after the meeting and offered to install the OS and the software on one of my lunch hours if she would approve the project. This is where I was told that under no circumstances was I to get involved in that process and that "managers didn't do that sort of work." I am pretty sure that she then launched into some annoyingly long story about her cat or one of her grandchildren or something, and probably asked why I had not yet found a way to fire EC or SB. I retreated to my office in defeat once again.

But this is in general how things work in ITS during the project charter process. You come to ITS to ask for things, and they smile sweetly while holding their fingers crossed behind their backs. Then they ask you to meet to discuss the details of your request, and they waste all of your time until you leave. Have you ever seen one of those shows where someone does something really stupid and everyone assures them that everything is fine, but then when they leave the room it erupts in laughter? That is what's going on when you, the customer leaves that project charter meeting. Chances are that the decision has already been made halfway through the meeting that you are not going to get what you asked for.

Yes they will put it on the list and yes they will enter the information into that piece of shit projects tracking application "request tracker" that GO mandated and built, but the chances of your project getting done are about as good as you getting out of giving head to Quasimodo's older brother without some serious brain trauma. Not likely.

Now to be fair to ITS and to the Business Relationship Team, and yes even to AH, there really are some customers who come to ITS with really stupid fucking ideas that were obviously excreted from someone's ass after they read a magazine article about this great new this or that that had been invented and really have no idea of what they fuck they really need. These people more then likely simply have some money to spend because its three weeks before they sweep all of the budgets, and they do not want to lose that money back into the general fund.

To those customers I say the following: Just because Billy Joe Bob Computer Geek in Bum Fuck USA invented a thing, does not mean that the taxpayers of Minnesota should pay for and implement such a thing. That thing is more than likely a piece of shit, and the taxpayers of Minnesota already have enough shit to deal with without you adding more shit to the pile. Let the funds go back into the general fund and maybe, just maybe if enough of you let all of that money go back into the general fund, those fuckers up the hill will get around to actually providing better services to those very same taxpayers – including yourself.

Besides, I am pretty sure that ITS more than likely already has a thing that will take care of your needs, and it will be far easier for you to get added to that thing, than to get a charter approved for a new one.

Also, there are many circumstances where a customer really does not know what they need or have even the slightest idea of how to accomplish these things. They simply come to the project charter meeting with an idea and then expect everyone to drop everything else to get it done. It then becomes up to ITS to not only figure out what they need, but how to design, implement, fund, and roll out that project. Unfortunately, these are usually the people who scream the loudest about ITS not being responsive to their needs, and to those people I say the following: “DO YER FUCKING HOMEWORK BEFORE YOU COME DOWN THERE ASKING FOR SHIT.”

It is not the job of ITS to hold your hand, wipe your ass, or otherwise figure out what the fuck you are talking about when you show up at that meeting. If you don’t have funding for a project, don’t expect anyone else to come up with it for you because it won’t happen. If you want a website, come to the meeting with a detailed diagram of what you want, who the website is for, what will be on it, does it need to be secure, will it gather data from other places, who will manage the website, what fucking color do you want it, yada yada, fucking yada. Do your homework well in advance, and if you don’t know anything about websites then bring someone with you who does. The goal here is to walk in there so fucking well prepared that the ITS people begin to look stupid. If you have been paying attention, I have already told you why your project probably won’t get done and there really isn’t much you can do about that. But if you walk in there with your balls out in the open, those people are just going to rip them off and show them to the next unprepared idiot who walks in the door as a warning.

Be prepared, know what you are talking about, and if you impress them, maybe, just maybe, one or two of them will at least fight for you. And if that doesn’t work, go befriend CZ. You may have to listen to her personal shit over and over again, but she will definitely skirt the rules for people she believes actually like her. Maybe if you are really nice to her, she will get your daughter a job whenever she comes home from college for the holidays. It works for MA.

The third kind of customer is the worst of all and one I call the bully. The bully walks around like they own the damned place and makes demands knowing that they have the clout to get them forced through the system. The bully customer has enough clout and resources to be able to manage their own technical infrastructure and tends to dictate what and when something happens on that infrastructure. The bully customer is one that comes into the project charter meeting with a list of demands and fully expects them to be implemented by ITS on their own schedule. The bully customer is one that will implement solutions and upgrades to infrastructure on a whim without consulting ITS or any other agency, even if it completely goes against the rules or affects another agency negatively.

They may install a client upgrade that will almost certain interfere with security systems or cause the users desktops to stop working, and then these organizations will come running to ITS demanding that ITS troubleshoot the problem without any knowledge of why the upgrade was performed or even of the fact that the upgrade had taken place at all.

While the unfortunate truth is that they may in fact own a small chunk of the place, as well as also be sleeping with the landlord, it is a well-known fact that ITS management still has the ability to reserve the right to refuse service to anyone for any reason. If you are one of these bullies, take note of the following items because they may save you a lot of trouble in the long run.

Rule number one. No one likes a bully or a smart ass. While bullies may at first seem to usually have the upper hand in any given situation, there are almost always ways to circumvent this level of control and those methods of circumvention are frequently utilized by ITS to slap the hand of any bully large enough to challenge them.

If you assume that one of these bully organizations comes forth with a list of demands, please understand that one of the ways that ITS will slow down the process is to call for a complete security audit. As I have indicated previously, security people are by nature paranoid individuals firmly lodged in the belief that the world is out to get them and that the only secure computer system is one that is turned off, unplugged and locked in a vault three hundred miles below the surface of the sun.

If you really want to throw a wrench in your project, start by screwing with any of the security teams or their manager. You can bet your big bully ass that by insisting that your project is the most important one in the world, and that ITS drop everything else to do it, the most immediate response will be one of the ITS directors screaming that the changes to your application you are proposing will compromise the security of the free world and end life on earth as we know it within weeks of implementation.

Rule number two. Demanding that your project be labeled as the most important one on the planet is also a sure way to ensure that several hundred thousand people will be sent an email informing them that due to your immediate need and demands, their project – which is currently about sixty-two seconds from completion – will need to be immediately halted and will not be completed until the year 2024. To these kinds of customers I say the following. You see my friends, it's not about the squeaky wheel getting the grease or jumping up and down and holding your breath until you turn blue. Its about finesse, and the ability to convince ITS that they really, really want to do your project because by completing your project right away, not only will they have saved all life in the universe, they will all receive immediate enlightenment, have gained a place at the right hand of whatever particular god they happen to serve, and feed a million starving children in Africa at the same time for less than thirty-two cents per day.

Whenever you get that particular project bug up your ass, pick up the phone and schedule a meeting with as many ITS people as possible. Tell them that you need their help and that you would really appreciate it if they would help you out. In other words, blow some serious smoke up their Asses because they love that shit. If you want to see ITS engineers sport some serious wood, spend a few minutes convincing each one of them that they alone are the only ones in the world who can solve your problem. And then sit back on your chair, fold your hands behind your back, and watch them run from the room foaming at the mouth on their way to collect enough people and resources to kiss your clever ass until it is sopping wet.

You can still do it the other way, and your project will more than likely eventually get done, but not as quickly and almost always at a cost of incredible aggravation and extra time on your part. Would you rather spend your time sucking down a cold one at the pub, or sending emails to your superiors explaining why ITS is dragging their feet?

You really need to understand that ITS is a large and complex organization. Unfortunately, this is due to the fact that management has pitted it against itself to the self-preserving benefit of maintaining control as opposed to getting things done. The people who work in engineering are those tasked with designing and implementing a solution once it has made it past all of the bullshit processes and procedures currently in place, and operations is tasked with the support and maintenance of those solutions once implemented.

The problem here is that no one likes to give up control of the ship when entering choppy waters. Everyone thinks that they can drive, steer, and control the boat better than everyone else. When you combine this with the fact that there is no actual guidance from management, and that priorities are decided utilizing the magic eight ball school of thought, what you end up with is a ship headed for the rocks and lots of people grabbing for the wheel. The five entities that make up ITS manage their priorities separately and expect that their priorities are the more important ones because CZ has told them all that they are and that everyone else should be cooperating with them to ensure that they are done.

It should have become apparent over the years that the system is broken and isn't going to be fixed by moving around the same old broken parts from manager to manager. It really should have become apparent that everyone can't be the most important dog in the yard. There has to be a hierarchy, some rules, and one final voice who lays down the law and prioritize the projects in some sort of sensible manner. At the moment, there are multiple voices, but all of them in one single head, and that isn't working very well, is it?

For the record, I am not indicating that I have any knowledge or proof of anyone suffering from schizophrenia, but… Oh, never mind, you get the idea.

You also have to realize that every few years the leadership of DHS changes and with that sort of change comes a quite different kind of priorities. A democratic commissioner that replaces a republican one is going to have different priorities, and will spend the first few months of his administration swapping out the people who disagree with him with people who do not. The old top priorities will then slide to the bottom of the list and new ones replace them at the top, and to be perfectly honest, if you think that at the lower rungs of DHS politics do not play a roll anymore, you are quite mistaken.

One thing that I always found interesting was that I never, ever heard anyone at DHS talk about politics. I think it's because everyone thinks that the place is bugged, and stating a political preference is more than likely the third thing that would get you fired or at least seriously on someone's shit list. I won't go there, as I am sure that we all know that all of those politician fuckers are liars no matter what side of the fence you are on. The bottom line is that whatever your priority, it could be a really good thing if at least a few of them kept a promise or two during the course of their positions.

And if you, my humble readers, have a project that you would like to see done, please fight for it, but be smart about it. The ITS staff really does have much to do and little time to do it. If you get them on your side, they will bust their tails to help you out. If you are a pain in the ass, you are pretty much just going to disappear into the black hole of politics and bullshit, and that, my friend, is never a fun place to be.

CHAPTER 4

BULLSHIT, CONJECTURE & SPECULATION:

(*Theirs not mine.*)

In this chapter we will delve into some of the major projects I was involved with at DHS. The projects that I will describe to you are all very interesting projects that range from those incorporating the needs of the internal customers to projects mandated by the governor's Drive to Excellence program.

Of course when no one is looking, everyone calls it the "Drive To Mediocrity," and that in itself should give you an idea of how worthwhile the people involved in these projects seem to think they are. It also goes to show that the people involved in these projects realize the frustration of certain policies and procedures and what it takes to achieve success.

Remember when I said that Information Technology had evolved over the years to include very specific sets of experience and technological expertise? It is important to remember that because it will help you understand how easily projects can become unruly, mismanaged, and occasionally, completely FUBAR when placed in the wrong hands. Also consider the fact that projects at DHS can costs many millions of dollars in time and effort, as well as the expense of the hardware and software required to run the infrastructure.

There is also the security infrastructure required to keep the previously mentioned scumbags from seeing things they shouldn't be seeing. A widely known fact in IT circles is that more than eighty percent of all security violations come from internal sources and not directly from the internet at large. Returning to my most-people-are-stupid theory, you can easily understand that this the case every time the news media announces that a laptop was stolen or lost with millions of confidential medical records or the secret to building a nuclear bomb on them.

I once found a public FTP site on the Internet that contained all of the personal information from a general in the US military. Using the information contained in those files, I could have gotten credit cards, loans, and all sorts of stuff, and I could have done it all from the comfort of my bedroom while sitting in my jammies.

When you add all of this up, a secure, well-performing technology solution can quickly become an unruly system that can eat up resources like a fat guy at an all you can eat buffet. The difference between the private sector and the state is that at the state, most of these projects are never cancelled when they fall seriously behind schedule because of the fact that they are covered by some local or federal mandate and because of management's innate desire to cover their Asses.

Remember that it's the system that is failing more likely than not and thus the end result is that more and more resources are simply thrown at a project until it is completed. How many times have you heard a news story about how many millions of dollars a certain government project is over budget? These projects become behind schedule and over budget because they are mismanaged and far too many mistakes are made.

Consider the 35W bridge collapse that happened in the spring of 2007 over the Mississippi. The winning vendor received a twenty-six million dollar bonus for completing the replacement bridge on time. I really wish someone would explain to me exactly what the point of that was. If I were to get quotes on a new addition to my house, I would take the bid from the guy who seemed reasonable and experienced in building additions of the kind I desire. In that bid, I would assume that the contractor has estimated his costs and the manpower required to complete the addition and approximately how long it would take him to complete the job. This is what I would base my decision on whether to hire that particular contractor. So if we assume that they had done their homework and provided a complete quote, why the hell would I need to pay him a bonus for completing the addition on time? In the case of that 35W bridge vendor, they received the twenty-six million dollar bonus for doing nothing more than what they indicated that they would do in the first place, and this really makes no sense to me at all, but what the hell.

I am going to guess that the reason the State of Minnesota agreed to pay them the bonus is more than likely the result of two issues that I will indicate right now. The people over at the department of transportation know that most people are stupid, but also that "shit happens." They also know that all of the political bickering and infighting would cause delays and other irrevocable roadblocks that would prevent the bridge from being completed on time.

They knew that the way government is structured balls will get dropped, incompetent people will be tasked with completing things that they know nothing about, and since the government can't be trusted to manage these things, they will have to rely on the contractor to be creative and push ahead through the bullshit politics in order to bring the project in on time. It also means that in their infinite political wisdom, someone up the hill decided on an exact date that the good people of Minnesota would tolerate the bridge being out and wanted to make damned sure that it was open by that date. I am also pretty sure that the fact that 2008 was an election year is somewhere in the mix there and that someone stuck driving an extra twenty miles per day to and from work is going to blame them for that fact and would have voted for someone else just to prove a point.

It should be said that I could honestly appreciate offering a bonus for a job well done, but twenty-six million fucking dollars? Give me a break. I'll leave a six pack or two in the back yard for the guys building my addition, but there is no way in hell I will offer to pay them an additional twenty percent of the job. I won't calculate how many children you could feed or provide medical services to, or how many roads would be repaired (bridge inspections anyone?) or how many schools in Minnesota could receive help, or cops hired, or whatever the case.

There is seriously something wrong with a system that rewards mediocrity to the tune of millions of dollars, and don't get me started on the chick that DOT fired because she chose to stay out east playing hide the salami with her boyfriend while everyone else was back in Minnesota risking their lives fishing bodies out of the Mississippi.

Anyway, the point of this chapter isn't to run off on some lengthy diatribe about how fucked up our government is... OK it is... but to talk about the projects that I worked on and why they will more than likely fail. All of the projects that I am going to talk about here are projects for the State of Minnesota or for ITS. You will recognize most of the players in this drama from previous chapters, which will almost certainly explain why these projects will fail. If those people are reading this then good, maybe you will go back and look at the situation and see how you could have done more to achieve success instead of sitting on your hands looking for someone else to blame for your incompetence.

Yes, I failed as well, but at least I tried to do something positive. I didn't write this book to make friends, but to ensure that going forward someone is aware of the pointless futility of expecting results from you. And if the end result is that you end up going away and getting another job because you are ineffective in your state job, then I'm not sorry about that at all. Besides, all those pizzas aren't going to deliver themselves.

As I told you previously, during my first weeks at DHS I held meetings with each of my direct reports to find out what they deemed to be some of the more serious issues in the department. I already had some serious doubts about the structure and viability of the department due to the many infuriating conversations that I had already had with CZ and GO.

One of the main complaints was that there was no real way to keep track of, coordinate, and assign information and tasks to the various departments and their staff. CZ attributed this lack of documentation to the staff being lazy and refusing to follow the rules. The rest of the staff and I attributed some of it to the fact that the procedures in place were an absolute waste of time. ITS had many places to store data and expected the staff to keep track of it all while being productive at the same time. I can explain this by asking that you pretend that you have several sets of tools in your house.

All of the metric tools are in one bucket, and all of the standard tools are in another. Also imagine that all of the screws, nuts and bolts, brackets, etc. are in yet another. Now imagine that each of these buckets is kept in a different place in your home and you need to install a new soap dispenser in the bathroom. First you go to the garage to get a screwdriver, then to the upstairs closet to get a screw, and then finally to the downstairs closet to get the drill. You gather all of these things in the bathroom that you intend to install the soap dispenser in, only to discover that the screws are too small and that the drill bit that you need is the wrong size.

You run around once more to exchange all of the tools. Then you discover that you can't locate the stud finder to make sure the dispenser is hung appropriately and that the standard screwdriver you grabbed is different from the Phillips screws that you originally grabbed and you still need a stud finder, so you spend an hour looking for that. Once you return to the bathroom, you realize that you can't find the screwdriver that you just got and after an exhaustive twenty-minute search you find it in your son's room where you left it when you stopped in there to tell him to take out the garbage. Finally, you are all set to install the soap dish, but you realize that its almost five o'clock and that you need to get started on dinner, and on and on and on. So by now you are getting the idea of what it's like trying to keep track of projects at DHS. You are required to spend more time getting ready to do something than it actually takes to do the thing in the first place. Data is stored all over the place. If someone would provide for a method to keep everything in one place, all of your tasks would be so much easier.

DHS has about twenty such places, as well as various forms, policies, and procedures for keeping track of such things. There have been so many forms to keep track of things at DHS, that everyone tends to use the one that they are most comfortable with. It's quite obvious that if they would simply provide a standard in all of these respects, life would be so much easier. At one of my meetings with CZ, I suggested that we use a tool that I was very familiar with by Microsoft called Sharepoint.

According to Microsoft, Sharepoint is "an integrated suite of server capabilities that can help improve organizational effectiveness by providing comprehensive content management and enterprise search, accelerating shared business processes, and facilitating information-sharing across boundaries for better business insight."

The simple version of this is that Microsoft Sharepoint is a really good place to collaborate on projects and an excellent place to keep all of your shit so that everyone can gain access to it without making themselves crazy.

I had implemented a Sharepoint site at my previous job and it really isn't all that complicated out of the box. The thing about a tool like this is that it pretty much comes stock out of the box with all sorts of templates and tools that you can get started with immediately, but that it also has a very complicated set of tools on the side that can be used to customize the product to your heart's desires. The trick is to roll out the project for people to use and then begin building on the stuff that is already there to customize the solution for individual departments and entire organizations. Trying to implement a completely customized solution for many different organizations at the outset is not only probably impossible, but futile as a product like this is designed to grow and mature with use and experience.

You may go to the grocery store with a list of things to buy, but inevitably, you will see something that may work better, be cheaper, or that you just find interesting, so you get that instead of the item on your list. This means that you have the ability to adapt and compromise to the current situation.

Enter MS into the project mix. CZ had told me that there was already a Sharepoint project in progress and that they had been working on it for well over a year. In fact, she actually thought it would be a great idea for me to get involved as maybe I could get the damned thing moving forward. At this point,

CZ still considered me the greatest thing since sliced bread, so she suggested that I call MS to set up a meeting. I set up the meeting, and I also talked to all of the other managers to determine what their needs might be for such a collaborating tool. I involved SB because she had done some extensive work with Sharepoint and I needed things to keep her busy anyway. I drew up a ten-page document on how the portal should look, what the approximate areas should look like and a tentative technical document outlining the hardware requirements. I distributed this document at the meeting, which included about ten people including SB and myself. That's the other problem with high visibility projects at DHS. As long as the project sits on some incompetent boobs desk, everyone is content to ignore it and leave it be. As soon as the project rises back into the light of day and becomes viable again, the vultures descend on it like flies to freshly laid dog shit.

As I said, at this point I was still CZ's flavor of the month, so everyone at that table pretty much expected me to pull this thing out of my ass no latter than lunch that afternoon. I was happy that they all seemed so enthusiastic about the prospect of actually getting this thing moving, but before we all started sucking each other's dicks right away, there was still a lot of work to be done. I gathered as much information as I could at that meeting and told them that I would draw up a plan based on this information and report back to them at the next meeting. As the meeting ended, MS informed me that they were truly happy to get this thing moving and that she was looking forward to the next meeting.

She also asked me how long this would take, and based on my experience, I informed her that I could see it happening within the next three to four months. Of course, I was still living under the delusional reality of thinking that people at DHS actually want their projects completed in a reasonable amount of time and to the benefit of the agency. As I have previously stated, most technology is easy, it's the people that are difficult. I also didn't know that MS was one of those people who hated SB with a passion and would fight tooth and nail to take her down, even if it meant delaying and pretty much fucking up the project in the process.

In no time at all, committees had been formed, investigative panels had been convened and there were no less than about two hundred thousand individuals and departments involved in this projects. Many different agencies were climbing the walls to become pilot programs for this newest collaborative tool, and the executive team had assigned many layers of responsibility, project sponsors, and other teams tasked with ensuring a smooth rollout. With so many people involved this project quickly became the unfunded cluster fuck it was inevitably going to be and all hell broke loose. I charged SB with making sure that all of the documents were well designed and that the system would be able to support the gazillion users it would invariably attract and be able to withstand a complete failure of the infrastructure in case some asshole blew up the building. She had done this well, and things began to move along nicely.

In short, we had designed an incredibly well laid out system pretty much capable of surviving a nuclear blast. We provided diagrams of the system and worked with the other agencies to ensure that everyone who needed to use the system could in fact use the system with no capacity issues. All we asked for in exchange was for MS and the project management team to lay out the system for us so that we could know how to build it and for the executive team to coral agencies interested in working to define and implement the system. It wasn't very long before all of those people who were only interested in their own interests and priorities crawled out of the woodwork to throw huge political wrenches in the works.

The web supervisor BP insisted that the site be compliant with the Americans with disabilities act, which is a noble issue and one that I readily agreed with. I asked him to provide us with the specifications for the site and told him that we would design the system around those specifications. He refused, stating that there were no actual specifications, and that we would just have to ask him for them. Yes, this son of a bitch stood there and told me that there were no specifications for a law that was mandated by the federal government and that the state was required to follow, which was of course absolute bullshit.

I asked him if any of the other DHS sites were ADA compliant and was told no, but that this one had to be. He ensured that he could keep his foot in the door by copying the office that managed the disabilities programs to tell them that we were intending on building a site that was not compliant, so they got involved and then also refused to provide us with the specifications that they demanded we follow. I searched the web and found the specifications and provided them to SB for implementation. BP then went off and found a company that made ADA compliant templates for Sharepoint and threw those into the mix. Of course, the templates he found were not compatible with our version of Sharepoint and would not be ready for at least six months.

The DHS commissioner's communications office got involved because they wanted to ensure that absolutely no information that they provided to DHS would be duplicated on the Sharepoint site. I knew this was mostly in fear that the DHS intranet would more than likely become obsolete if they could get the same information on the cool new website as opposed to the old shitty one, which was also not ADA compliant by the way. Many meetings were scheduled to ensure that no information would be duplicated and that someone in the commissioner's communications office would have the authority to review all information posted to the site before it was posted. I had several issues with this because the nature of most of the information that ITS would be posting would be security related and not for public consumption. If you think back to my statement about most security violations coming from the inside of an organization, you know that there would be absolutely no way in hell that we were going to allow them access to this information. Of course, this all had to be discussed in detail over a series of months and many meetings which caused additional delay.

On and on this all went, as well as other delays and interference from any department that felt that they would be entitled to dictate the direction of this project until the project was many months behind schedule and really had indeed become FUBAR. The agencies involved in the pilots wanted to ensure that they would receive top priorities in any management or changes of their site even though they professed to not having the resources or knowledge to develop the site and in spite of the fact that I had laid out a detailed plan which was to have the Applications Development Team implement any changes that they would like.

CSED was now banging at the door insisting that they be the lead on the project because they had already, but unofficially, implemented a Sharepoint site. This was one of the programs that CSED had "piloted" for the agency but then managed to insist that they could no longer work without it, and thus it had become the defacto standard for collaborations tools within their agency. CZ was insisting that ITS be the main managers of the projects because they had designed, built and paid for the infrastructure, as well as the fact that we were the only people on the planet who could successfully implement such a complicated infrastructure.

Building Services insisted that they be the project sponsors because the project spanned many different agencies and that all agency tools were usually put to them to manage. All of this and much more caused incredible delays in the project. All I had wanted to do was set up a site so that we would have a place to coordinate our efforts between agencies, and everything got all fucked up because people wanted to protect their own silos.

MS absolutely refused to work with all of the agencies to provide us with any sort of logical diagram even though SB kept asking for this information. MS, of course, spent her time complaining that SB was simply being a pain in the ass and requesting information that she did not need. She also made a huge deal about anything that did not fall directly under her purview. Once, after she had received yet another request from SB asking for the site diagrams we had been waiting for six months for, I actually received an email from MS worded in the following way: “I thought we were going to keep that bitch on a short leash.”

I couldn’t fucking believe my eyes when I read that, and all because SB was asking for something which was needed and required to design the site. MS didn’t want to provide it because it was SB that was asking for it and wasn’t going to provide it as long as SB was involved in the project. She continued this sort of behavior even though if I had pulled SB off the project, all work would have come to a screaming halt. To be honest, now that I think about it, I can’t remember if she used the actual word Bitch, but the rest of it is absolutely true, and I am pretty sure she did use the word in her email.

The irony of this all was that when I did eventually pull SB off the project, the first thing that DA, who was her replacement, asked for was a logical diagram of the site – which of course MS immediately provided to him. I am still unsure as to why she didn’t just provide the fucking thing in the first place in order to further a project that she professed was so important to her and to the agency. And so the project floundered on like this for months and months with little being achieved in the way of progress, until I finally got fed up and refused to participate in anything except the spirit of the program, as CZ is so fond of calling the passive aggressive behavior so rampant at DHS. From that point on, whatever MS asked for, I gave her, which had the net effect of turning over the project to her in its entirety.

We provided basic support services for the infrastructure and she began sending out emails every week or so espousing the incredible amount of progress that they were making now that SB was gone, which was of course complete bullshit. No progress was being made, and we had in fact taken two steps backwards.

In August of 2007 the executive team declined the funding for the Sharepoint project due to lack of progress and more than likely the knowledge that the project was simply going nowhere. The project was allowed to die a slow painful death, and it is my understanding that the infrastructure that we built is still there and people are still poking around in it.

The bottom line is that it what began as a great and noble project, which would have benefited the agency enormously, turned to shit because of lousy project management. ITS still does not have any way to track projects and it's associated documentation and the agencies once so eager to participate in the pilot program all backed out because they assumed correctly that the project was going nowhere and would not be supported.

The second project that I will talk about is the Email Storage & Retention project, which is a project also begun before I arrived at DHS. This project was centered around the fact that DHS management wanted the ability to control exactly what emails were kept and for how long. Depending on who you asked, there were really other reasons for this, but my guess right out of the gate was that the ability to control the amount of information that could summoned for legal purposes was more to the point. The reasons for this are three-fold. First of all, most people are pack rats and if they are not given particular guidelines about what you can and cannot save, most people will just save everything.

This is due to the basic assumption that most of us make in thinking that we are so important that our every word and action should be archived in perpetuity. This pack rat problem becomes exponentially worse with technological solutions such as email. An email created by one individual which is then sent to ten other people and then forwarded by those ten people to ten other people, and so on has the ability to blossom into a sea of emails which will raise the storage requirements of an agency very quickly.

That one stupid email announcing the birth of the receptionist's newest spawn, complete with a picture of said spawn, grows exponentially when everyone forwards the email to either extol the attractiveness or outright butt-ugliness of said spawn. But for the sake of argument, let's say that said single email is actually about state business. That email, having been forwarded a few hundred times, now takes up a considerable amount of space and when you multiply this by a few hundred thousand emails created and received by state employees every week you can imagine the storage requirements necessary to house all of those pictures of that one ugly baby.

On a side note, why does everyone think that his or her baby is the cutest in the world? All babies are ugly little alien creatures with the single caveat that some are uglier than others. All of them look the same for the most part, and strolling around the office with pictures of them only serves to make most people ill. I would be more impressed if someone were to stroll around the office with video of the conception, and what I really want to do the next time someone shoves a baby picture in front of me is to explain exactly how "not-so-much," the baby isn't really cute, and then barf on the hand extending the picture, but I digress.

Anyway, the other reason is that the state has very specific policies regarding dissemination of state information which is to say that almost all state information is public information, it is the state's responsibility to provide access to state information when requested, and finally, the state shall provide this information in a complete and timely manner when requested.

The loophole in the system is that if the state were to implement a policy dictating date retention periods of a relatively short nature, they are allowed to simply tell the person knocking at the door asking for that information that it falls outside of the state mandated retention period and that that data is no longer available. When receiving a legal demand for documents, they usually send out an email asking a few key people to search for this data. Obviously, not very many people bother to actually search for this data so the request is responded to with limited or distorted information. The best thing to do were they to actually desire to comply with this request is to ask ITS to search for the data on the network.

This would more than likely result in the requested information being provided, but the ITS director has incorrectly informed the agency that it is impossible to search for all of this information or that such a search would be too resource intensive and would cost gazillions of dollars to perform, which is, of course, all completely untrue. Obviously, this has the added benefit of covering up all of the corrupt activities and lack of progress on projects because such a request may simply be ignored if the data should reside somewhere else on the network because no one remembers exactly where they put that document so no one bothers to look for it.

For example, if the DHS commissioner was to hire an executive receptionist at an extremely high salary who according to everyone else who works there seems to have no real duties, other than to accompany the commissioner on overnight business trips, some of this information might show up in a document or email or two and would be subject to the laws mandating discovery.

If, of course, these emails no longer existed, then there would be no actual proof of said inappropriateness, and everyone goes home happy at the end of the day. Or if someone was to spent state dollars making “business” trips out east to see a boyfriend when entire bridges are collapsing back home, and their manager had been ignoring such behavior, there might not be a record of such activities. For the record, I mention this particular scenario as an example only and acknowledge that I personally have no proof of such inappropriate behavior by any state employee or DHS commissioner except for that which has been reported in the news.

Anyway, DHS had tentatively purchased a system designed by Hewlett Packard to store and manage these emails and of course EC had only purchased a part of the system from his favorite vendor because the budgeting process would fail to notice such a large purchase if it were done in small parts. Apparently, they had spent the last year trying to get the system implemented, and EC now came to me to request approval to purchase the remaining system to the tune of about a half-million dollars.

CZ in between a story about her divorce and her new neighbor's garden blew a gasket when she saw the invoice and asked me if there were a way to get the cost down. I informed her that the easiest way would be to just set retention limits on the email server and that emails created before a certain period would auto magically disappear. Of course, this wasn't acceptable to her and I was sent off to find a way to get the cost down. I did eventually find another product by another vendor, which did the same thing for less than the cost of what they had already spent, and because the HP hardware had not yet been fully implemented we could send it back without any penalties. EC, of course, had a complete cow because I was going to go with a vendor that he had no relationship with.

This would be the first time, but not the last that I told him in no uncertain terms that, while I understood his point, it was too fucking bad, and we were going with the alternate solution. I called HP and told them to pick up their overpriced solution. This was almost a year ago and I believe that it is still sitting there. I guess they need to figure out how to put the product back in inventory and recover the kickbacks without anyone figuring out on either side that the rules had been skirted to the benefit of vendors and state employees.

This newly christened project went pretty well until SOS got involved. SOS is the agency I talked about before and one that the powers that be had instructed ITS to incorporate into their network infrastructure five years ago. It should be noted at this point that SOS plays the fuck you game very well and managed to throw up all sorts of roadblocks in getting this product implemented. Issues that were non-issues were brought up and then committeed to death as often as possible. SOS refused us access to their network and insisted that they were to be in charge of the project even though the executive team had mandated that the project be controlled by central office.

While the installation on our side went pretty much without a hitch, the SOS install was brought to an immediate halt due to a series of problems, issues, and complications which were all brought on by their refusal to cooperate in getting the project implemented. I found it amusing that emails were sent flying at the beginning of this project informing pretty much everyone on the planet that they had no knowledge of this project and needed a few months to investigate and test the product when they had had a representative sitting at the very table where we discussed all aspects of the project in detail.

Of course every time there was a complication they sent out emails to pretty much everyone in state government informing them that they could not meet our timeline because everything was so fucked up, and that we had simply sprung this project on them with no advance warning. They would bring up issues to be resolved, and we would offer to come out and fix those issues if they would give us access to their network, which if course they refused to do under the guise that the people who needed to be there were on vacation or dead, or jerking off in the back room or something.

In the meanwhile, they would fire off another email to another million or so people stating that we were unable to solve their problems and that the problem would have to be delayed a few hundred years or so. This was quite simply the most fucked up sense of self-entitlement I have ever experienced in my twenty plus years in IT. Due to the nature of the game, and the fact that I was still a newbie, they were able to get away with it. This is one of the examples I mentioned earlier when I stated that there are ways to manipulate the system, if one truly desired to do so. It is often said that if you mess with the bull, you get the horn.

We got the whole fucking head on this one and this was a mandated project, with go ahead signatures from pretty much everyone, and yet they still got away with playing games and delaying the project. The project was eventually implemented in the summer of 2007, or at least the first part of it was after much delay and political wrangling. It also became at least part of one of the things that seemed to convince CZ that I was not "engaged" in her distorted view of the world, when I told everyone that we could retrieve the data that MPR had requested.

I didn't mention previously that I had done at least one of the searches that they had requested and kept the data after CZ instructed me to loose it. (EMAIL FROM CZ AT THE END OF BOOK) Once CZ had released me from the hell that was DHS, I provided that information to MPR, as well as information on exactly how they should request the data that they wanted and where in the system this information would be located. As I write this, I am not sure what will have become of that information, but as I know that the commissioners office was filtering that data before I left, I hope there is a discrepancy large enough to hang CZ's ass out to dry. She had also asked me to kill the mechanism that served to track all of this data, which I conveniently forgot to do before I left. I hope she never realized it, which would mean that it is still there and available for gathering should someone decide to request it.

Email systems serve as a great place to store data because it is the fasted way to send and receive information at very little ongoing costs and since the information is already there, most people simply let it sit there forever. This is either a good thing or a very bad thing depending on your point of view. From a company's viewpoint, keeping data around that might serve to identify some sort of wrongdoing is a bad thing, just ask the ENRON guys. Most companies have solved this problem by implementing policies that forbid the long-term storage of such information.

Knowing this, the inevitable result was that congress got involved and made it a crime to destroy certain types of financial data and mandated national policies and procedures that instruct companies on the correct way to store this data. As there are always loopholes in the system, those loopholes are being tested by DHS at this very moment to avoid accountability issues. Apparently, there was a legislator up at the state capital that suggested all data be archived according to specific state standards, and almost everyone there had an absolute cow about it. While I applaud his conviction and honesty, I seriously doubt if he will be reelected for having the nerve to suggest that everyone be held accountable for their actions. This is, of course, America, and if GW's White House can get away with destroying data to cover up its miss-deeds, I have little hope for our local government being held to any higher standards.

The Enterprise Email Consolidation project was one mandated by the governor's supposed Drive to Excellence program. Before I get into the meat of this one, I would like to mention to the governor that it really would be excellent if he would actually watch what the hell is going on in these state agencies instead of spouting bullshit and limited technical knowledge just to get elected. I know that he ran partially on the guise of his understanding technology because he used to run a technology company. He failed to mention that the technology company that he ran went out of business while under his control. The company that I was working for at the time was utilizing their services and received a letter one day informing us that we had two weeks to find another service provider. Maybe he really meant that he ran a technology company into the ground, and a last minute editing mistake by one of his writers accidentally dropped the last part of that sentence.

Anyway, this project was by far the most enjoyable and the one that was the least pain in the ass during my stay at DHS. I am going to contribute this to the fact that there were no DHS people involved in the process except for myself. I only bring it up here to show that it is indeed possible to be productive and provide a decent service in spite of the rules and regulations that bind state government to the wall. It is also the story that explains when and why I was asked to falsify data to another agency by my director.

One of the edicts of the Drive to Excellence initiative is to combine some of the many services each state agency provides to its employees into larger consolidated solutions which will serve to enhance services, collaboration between agencies, and save money. By combining these technology solutions, the state would see a decrease in costs by increasing negotiation power over the vendors and reducing overall maintenance and support costs. Most technology solutions are sold with some sort of licensing agreement, as well as additional costs which tend to cover technical support and any upgrades to the systems that might be released by the vendors. These additional costs tend to run in the fifteen to twenty percent range, which can substantially increase the cost of these solutions. When you have several hundred agencies who previously were tasked with providing these services for their own needs, it is logical to assume that they all made decisions on which solution made the best sense for them at the time. That also means that the state is paying more than once for different but same solutions, and I will explain these costs in the following way.

There are several enterprise solutions on the market all provided by very large corporate entities and these entities are in direct competition with each other. There is always a server level back end to these solutions, which controls the ins and outs of email distribution, as well as a storage facility to house all of the data. There is a single cost for the server software, and the server software is then licensed by how many users you wish to have connected to the server system. These costs can vary greatly. Usually, a single organization has the initial cost of the server product, and then license costs for each of its users. At the state, this cost is replicated many times over because of the many disparate systems that have been implemented. That is to say that each agency pays for a different server product and then the user licenses for each product. If you were to combine all of the agency email systems, then you would reduce the costs that the state is paying for a particular solution by reducing the server licenses and you only pay for the one product. In addition, you also reduce the support costs of these systems because you no longer require several people with distinctly different knowledge and experience to manage these systems. There is also one additional benefit of combining these systems which is that any of the major companies that provide enterprise email systems would give their left tit to be known as the one enterprise solution chosen by the State of Minnesota and is therefore likely to bend over backwards to be the chosen vendor. While this is a very basic explanation of how it all works, you get the idea in a nutshell, and the same is true for most of the other solutions such as telephones, fax, software, printers, etc. in this case, more is almost always better than less. If you have one solution you have only one cost.

At first glance, the more observant of you will realize that while this theory is completely logical and makes complete sense for the state as a whole. It is less logical if you are one of those agencies who are mostly interested in justifying their existence and protecting their particular silos. Of course, the smaller agencies were all ready to jump on board because as a whole, they tend to run on a shoestring budget and are more than happy to pay a few dollars to someone else to manage their solutions than to pay lots of money for some geek to sit in the back room with his thumb up his ass in case something stops working. DHS is one of the larger agencies, and having implemented their own email solution, they will fight tooth and nail to ensure that in the eyes of its management, nothing makes less sense than turning over their systems to OET, even if the truth is something completely different.

CZ volunteered me to participate in the Enterprise Email project, which is essentially to say that she wanted a spy in their midst who would report back to her and give her enough information to be able to counteract any forward moves they made in what she more than likely deemed to be a hostile takeover. I already mentioned that Bacon Boy and CZ were terrified that OET would swoop in and assume command, regardless of how much money it might save the state. The governor needs to realize that the best thing in the world would be for them to do exactly that. ITS is managed by a bunch of serial misfits who will only strive to provide services to the agencies requesting it if those services are forcibly yanked from the ITS director's ass. Since DHS received more that a quarter of the state's budget, I can imagine that there will be several hundred millions of dollars saved over a short period of time by eliminating all of the bullshit meetings, political wrangling, and departmental posturing that only serves to protect the jobs of its incompetent management.

Anyway, I began by attending weekly meetings where technical representatives were present from all of the major agencies in the state. I won't go into all of the details about the process involved in designing such a system, as it is pretty much guaranteed to bore the shit out of you. Let's just say that coordinating a project of this nature is quite a long process involving much technical information gathering, defining requirements for many disparate agencies, developing scoring methodologies, and on and on. You end up with a really long document, or "Request For Proposal," (RFP) which serves to outline all of the requirements necessary to implement such a large statewide email system. This went on for many months until the final document was set to be posted on the website for all of the vendors to review and respond to with a proposal meeting all of the requirements. I and the other people involved in this process really did bust our asses in an attempt to design a solution that would meet the requirements of as many agencies as possible, and I was very happy to have sat down with other technical people and work through all of the issues as they became apparent. It wasn't perfect by any means, but opinions were listened to, debated, and respected. Everyone was given a chance to provide information from their agency, and that, my friend, is what collaboration is all about. DHS could learn many things from such a process.

It took many months to get through this process meeting. It was only for a few hours one day per week, and each week, I was expected to provide a report to CZ about what went on at these meetings, which I did. Every time there was something she didn't like, I was subjected to being grilled in all of the ways we could avoid transferring control to OET. Every once in a while, in response to the questions we came up with on the evaluation team, OET would send a questionnaire to the CIO so that we could keep working. JB would send the questionnaire to me, and CZ would sit down with me and tell me exactly how to answer each question which she would then return to JB as if they came from me and JB would send them back to OET.

These questions were usually requesting information having to do with level of effort and cost of maintaining our own email solution. CZ would task me with finding out what our costs were concerning our email solution and then once provided would take issue with them and we would sit down and massage these numbers until they met her particular delusion of what we would be paying for services should OET provide them. The truth of the matter was that should OET provide these services, DHS would be paying considerably less than we were paying and require much less support staff, but CZ didn't want to hear that, and thus I was required to falsify those numbers every time they were requested.

Servers that could have been eliminated once OET had started to provide email services suddenly became crucial to DHS and so the costs would remain firmly in the DHS column. Support people whose main job was email suddenly became indispensable because now all of a sudden they had other tasks to work on and DHS would disappear into obscurity if they were to go away. This went on for weeks and these numbers were sent to OET as gospel and with my name on them even though they were based on absolute bullshit logic. Of course, I couldn't tell OET this because CZ would have my nuts in a wringer if I did.

Fortunately, or unfortunately depending on your point of view, this was about the time that I had figured out that CZ and I were never going to be able to see eye to eye on these things and that bacon boy was already in full swing in his quest to see me ousted from ITS for not kissing his ass properly. Armed with all of this information, I started taking a new tact on all of the immoral and more than likely illegal things she was asking me to do. I started ignoring her requests until the last minute so that she wouldn't have time to ask me to falsify the numbers and this really pissed her off. On one occasion, I gave her the numbers less than an hour before her meeting in the commissioner's office, and she then insisted that I attend the meeting with her to explain the change in the numbers. I attended this meeting and in fact rode up on the elevator with her, which was to say at least a little disconcerting. I already knew that this woman was going to have my balls for lunch, and so I just held my ground on the numbers refused to change them.

The explanation that I gave at the meeting was that we on the Enterprise Email team had finally addressed all of the remaining issues, which had changed the numbers substantially, which was only partially true. I wanted, of course, to stand up and shout that these had been the numbers all along, but that she had been making me change them to serve her purposes, but of course I couldn't do that. She spent the better part of the meeting stumbling through this new information, glaring at me, and whenever someone asked me a question, she would interrupt me to provide her own answers.

If looks could have killed, my head would have exploded right then and there, but she had to maintain her relative cool. Instead, she searched her tiny, little, uninformed and incredibly pissed off mind for something else to inhibit this project. The one thing that she came up with was that OET was not a HIPPA certified organization.

Of course, this had been addressed already and of course OET was quite capable to providing HIPPA level security as they already did for other agencies, but this was the only thing she could grab on to and thus she stuck to it. This works well when you are presenting information to non-technical people and those non-technical people are relying on you as the sole source of that information. I wasn't about to mention this because I am pretty sure that she would have reached across the table and taken my head off right then and there before launching into yet another anecdote about her cat or something.

She was incredibly pissed, and there was no way I was going to escape without a royal ass chewing. So once the meeting was over, and all the way down in the elevator, I listened as she told me how disappointed she was, and how I had embarrassed her, the agency, my mother, god, something about her rose garden, but also how angry JB would be, and that she "just didn't know what to do about this." I already knew about this and in my head I kept repeating my new mantra, "fuck you stupid bitch, fuck you stupid bitch." When we got back to her office, I dropped my pants, bent over and took it like a man, but a man contented in the fact that he had finally stood up for himself to the class bully and had won. By the way, I iterate that I was speaking metaphorically about the whole dropping my pants thing for those of you still unable to recognize my kind of sarcasm at first glance.

CZ didn't speak to me for several days, but every time I saw her she gave me that same disappointing look that your cat gives you when you and whomever you happen to be bumping uglies with start having sex in the bed they were recently taking a nap on. It is a look of abject disappointment and indignation. It is the look that says in no uncertain terms, "how fucking dare you, you inconsiderate bastard." I was a happy man at this point. I knew I was a goner, but fuck her. I knew she could take me down, but if I was going down, I was going to go down in my own way and with as much of my pride in tact as possible.

I managed to get through the process and I threw OET hints whenever I could about the fact that the numbers they were basing information on might not be as useful as they thought and that they should take anything they get from DHS with a grain of salt. OET already knew this, of course, but confirmation is always a good thing. I also began saving pretty much all of my emails especially the ones where she indicated her disappointment in the numbers I was giving her.

The other point I wish to mention in regard to this project is that there are some inherent difficulties in the way the state decides on contracts. We received about twelve responses to the original proposal request for Enterprise Email. Two of them were thrown out immediately because they failed to provide the requested information about the company or for some other reason. There are detailed requirements mandated to ensure that the playing field is kept level or at least that the playing field seems to be level. The rules contain things like number of employees, number of minorities in an organization requesting state contracts, years of experience, etc.

This is probably a good thing as it serves to keep Billy Joe Bob's House of 'Puters and Taco Salads from receiving state contracts due to the fact that he once owned a commodore 64 computer. On the other side, it ensures that only large, experienced companies can bid for state projects and those basically consist of companies more than capable of playing the games required to complete government work and who can throw resources at a project when it becomes irrevocably over budget and behind schedule.

After about three months, the number of proposals was cut down to about six or seven for one reason or another. Some of the proposals were just horribly inadequate and so were eliminated for lack of expertise, failure to provide required information in specific areas, or for not meeting criteria that the RFP stated was essential and would cause them to be disqualified. There are always vendors who, after being disqualified, will bitch, piss and moan about the fact that they didn't win the contract, but this is to be expected.

A sufficiently funded vendor can in fact hold up a project for months or even years with appeals, but this is rarely done especially in a case where that vendor has other state contracts and wishes to continue working on state contracts in the future. As I have previously implied, there are almost always ways around the system and a vendor who causes too much noise can quickly become persona non-gratis so most of them bitch quietly in the background and then give up their request for re-consideration.

Also keep in mind that the RFP that we came up with to outline the scope of the project was about two-hundred pages and extremely detailed with regard to what the state requirements were for an enterprise email system. Every detail of every aspect of every requirement was considered, debated, discussed, and inevitably given a score as to its importance. We eventually narrowed the list down to four top vendors and then invited those four back in for a verbal presentation. This would be the point where a vendor has a chance to really shine and give us their best effort in knowledge and in costs. There were of course the vendors who did bitch, piss, and moan about the fact that they had not been chosen to come back. Lawsuits were threatened, feet were stomped and breaths were held but they eventually got over it and went away. Of the remaining four vendors, two were excellent, one was pretty good, and the fourth was only there because they tried to buy the contract by pretty much giving the software away for free.

The larger vendors can do this because they know that once their foot is in the door that it would be very difficult for us to dislodge them and because the state is required by law to take cost as the top consideration in accepting most proposals. All state contracts have an expiration period and there was nothing in the contract that would stop the vendor from raising the price of the software at the end of the contract to more than make up for having given the software away in the first place. Given that this vendor would not have even been in the top six or seven if the decision were based only on technical merit, many meetings were held in an attempt to figure out how to deal with this issue. On one hand, you have a vendor who fails in almost every area except for cost, but that cost puts them at the top of the list. On the other hand, if we had accepted the rules as gospel and to the exact letter of the law, the state would have had to agree to and implement a system that was substandard, barely met all of the criteria, and did not include all of the requested services from a vendor that more than likely would have fallen short of the desired criteria.

I am going to go back to the 35W bridge thing again because that seems to be a similar situation where everyone is running around bitching that the proposal that was eventually accepted was not the cheapest proposal submitted. You can be sure that the losing vendor is the one who leaked the fact that their proposal was cheaper, but the truth of the matter is that cheaper is not always better. All of the details are considered in a proposal like this and the details are what can make or break a project. Maybe their proposal was cheaper because they were going to use a lesser grade of cement or that they were going to use only five pins per square foot instead of the ten that the winning vendor was going to use. I don't have access to this information, but knowing how the process works, I am going to give DOT the benefit of doubt and say that they probably made the best choice for the state of Minnesota with regard to what vendor to select.

They had better have made the correct choice because heads will roll if that bridge has any issues in the next three hundred years or so. I also want to state for the record that although this may seem in direct conflict with my original statement about the state wasting money, and I hope you realize that, if you think about it, there is a difference between the cheapest and the best. Ask yourself if you want the cheapest bridge or the best bridge. Yes, it's a really great thing if the best happens to be the cheapest as well, but that is rarely the case in bridge building.

Fortunately for us, the vendor solved our issues with their proposal by showing up at the proposal meeting, giving a substandard proposal, not being able to sufficiently answer technical issues with their responses, and failing to meet all of the specified RFP criteria. This eroded their points enough to remove them from the top spot and the points were reallocated to the remaining vendors. Since state law mandates that the cost be at least forty percent of the decision making process, the state really dodged a bullet on that one, however this whole process exemplifies a governmental system that can often work against itself. The members of that team worked very hard to provide a solution that would meet as many of the needs of state employees as possible and that also met the criteria originally set out at the beginning of the project. It was actually a pleasure to be a part of that team and DHS could learn quite a few things from them.

The next project that I will talk about is the Systems Monitoring project and a fine example of how bacon boy distorts the facts to maintain control and all with the blessing of the ITS director.

One morning, after I had been at DHS about a month, we started getting complaints from users that they either could not access the internet or that most of the websites they were trying to access would not come up. After some investigation, it was determined that the DNS scopes on the servers had been deleted. DHS servers keep track of where things are located either on a local network or on the Internet. Websites aren't really names so much as they are addresses. For example if you type amazon.com into your browser, your computer goes to the DNS server and asks it for the address of amazon.com.

If your DNS server does not know where amazon.com lives, it will ask another DNS server for the information, and then another, and another until it locates the address for amazon.com which is 72.21.206.247. Once it knows the address for amazon.com it gives it to your browser and your browser goes there on its own utilizing various protocols and criteria I won't get into for obvious reasons that are beyond the scope and purpose of this book. DHS has about seven of these servers in case one or more of them goes down and all of these DNS servers keep information about what websites they know about and their respective addresses. This means that if you were to go into one of these servers and delete the information for amazon.com, that server will tell all of the other servers to forget about it as well. That morning apparently someone had gone into one of the servers and told it to forget about all of the web addresses that it knew about, and that server, as it is supposed to do, informed all of the other ones, and they forgot everything as well because that is what they are supposed to do.

The net result of this was that anytime someone on the network tried to access another server on the network, the DNS servers simply shrugged their shoulders and returned an error proclaiming ignorance. The good thing is that on a properly configured network, servers have the ability to discover other servers on their own, and thus the address database is quickly rebuilt as the servers receive requests that tell them to go out and find the requested information. I was more than slightly annoyed because in my twenty plus years, I have never, ever seen a DNS server have any sort of internal error that would cause it to delete all of its data on its own and so it was obvious to me that someone had deleted the DNS information either accidentally or on purpose.

I asked my security team to review the security logs on the server to determine who had done this. I won't go into all of the details about how DHS has its servers set up or the fact that most of the logs that track this sort of information are randomly kept and unorganized, or it was simply not available. According to my staff, this information was not available, or they did not want to give it to me to protect one of their own. Let's give them the benefit of doubt and simply say that it was not available. I also found it incredibly interesting that this data was also conveniently not available from the nightly backups, but was just something I would have to deal with later.

Once we had rebuilt the servers, I started a project charter to implement a system for monitoring all internal systems so that in the future we would be notified of this sort of information that would be required to keep track of what was going on the network. I spent the next four months working on this project, assigning resources, meeting with vendors, and designing the comprehensive monitoring system that should have been in place in the first place. I followed all of the rules, held the proper meetings, and involved all of the appropriate people in the pre-defined processes. Bacon boy ignored all of the meeting invites, and in fact generally ignored all aspects of this process, even when asked if he had an opinion on any aspect of the project. I just assumed that he had other things on his mind or didn't particularly find this project interesting at all. When we had all of our ducks in a row, I submitted the EIOR to purchase the products to CZ.

As I later found out, CZ runs most things like this through bacon boy anyway, but I wasn't worried about it because if he were all that interested, he would have attended the meetings on one of the two or three days that he happen to be in the office, and I fully expected this project to move forward without any problems. There were additional incentives to move this project forward as well because we had received several requests from customers asking us to provide monitoring of their systems so that they could be aware of any pending services issues and CZ had mentioned the need for this system several times over my first few months at DHS.

This was only the first of many of my projects that BB killed by telling CZ that he was not in agreement with the proposed solution and that since he had not been in the loop in the development process, the whole thing would have to be started all over again.

I had just spent four months working on a fantastic project that served no other purpose than to provide system wide monitoring and security benefits to the agency and that asshole killed it with the wave of a pen and that fruitcake of a director allowed him to do so without consulting me or asking even one question of me or my team. By now I was wondering what the fuck I was there for anyway if all projects were subject to the whims of one single contractor. This also provided an incredible amount of credence to my assumptions that I had been hired were under false pretenses and was not actually there to provide any management or leadership.

It was becoming quite clear that I was only there to take the heat in dealing with problem agencies and employees. All of the issues that CZ and BB had been unable to deal with were passed on to me, and the fact that I had not been willing to stick my neck out for them was becoming more of a liability than BB had counted on. This was also about the time I started simply agreeing with whatever he wanted, as it was then quite obvious that it really didn't matter what I wanted or the fact that I had extensive experience in implementing enterprise level applications and that I had been hired to do so. So, yet another project that would have greatly benefited the agency, its internal customers and the Minnesota public at large died a horrible death. This project was still on the shelf the day I left and most likely will not have been completed as of the date this book hits the shelves.

I understood that BB wanted to preserve his sweet smelling position as project manager and well-paid contractor for DHS. I do not understand why the director tasked with providing those services allowed him to circumvent the processes, the people, and the good of the state employees to his own benefit without any repercussions at all. I sincerely hope that one day it is discovered that they have a secret love child or something because no other explanation would have made any sense. On the other hand, although that is one possible answer to this mystery, it wasn't my impression that was the kind of work he was hired to do.

The final project that I wish to talk about is the SOS integration project. From my understanding, this project had been going on for about five years and had gotten exactly no-where. The project was a mandate by the commissioner to integrate all of the DHS agencies into one big conglomeration of technology. I realize that even though this kind of integration would serve to save money and reduce the level of resources required to run separate agencies, I also believe that the more obvious intent of such a project would be to consolidate additional power into the DHS central office.

Remember my statement about consolidating systems, the fact that by doing this you could save a lot of money on both resources and services, and then remember what I said about agencies exerting a considerable amount of effort in protecting their silos and protecting their positions. Now consider the fact that SOS is one of the state's largest agencies with about six thousand employees. If you add all of those things up, you end up with an agency that quite literally is large enough to maintain the ability to smile in your face while giving you the finger at the same time when asked to do something they do not desire to do.

As I have stated before, passive aggressive behavior runs rampant at DHS and although this methodology can be used to serve many purposes, the one that is most often utilized is that of the passive aggressive delaying tactic.

One method is that people practicing this methodology can tend to agree with you on one aspect and then immediately turn around and spread rumors about what is going on to instill panic throughout an agency. These rumors almost always have a "twist" to them, and it takes much effort to correct a misconception that spreads at the speed of email. As you all know, in life it often doesn't matter if said rumor is true or not, but that once said the rumor begins to spread around the office and people will spend considerable time and effort talking about, spreading, and enhancing such a rumor to fulfill their own purposes.

Meetings can be rescheduled for months to hold off unwanted conversations if the individuals who do not want to have the meeting are successful in insisting that many other people are necessary and that they be involved. If you get enough people involved this can last for years, as it is very difficult to get many people consistently together in the same room especially in an organization the size of DHS. This can work to your passive aggressive advantage as well; because if someone is required for a meeting and is unavailable for that meeting, then you simply have the meeting anyway and then you tell everyone that you need to confer with the missing individual later.

You then have another meeting to have all of those questions answered from the previously missing individual while using that meeting to incorporate additional roadblocks into the process, but you get the idea. A very experienced, passive aggressive, bullshit procrastinator can keep things that they do not want to do in the air for years. Anyone who has been at DHS for many years is more than likely very experienced in this method of non project management.

As I have said, the project was intended to combine these two distinct and separate entities into one comprehensive one, but the problem is that SOS was having none of it. Apparently a few years back, SOS went through a major reorganization and many jobs were lost, complete agency entities were eliminated, and those people who survived this original cleansing remembered it well and quickly decided to dig in and fight any attempts at an additional reorganization. They had been successful in fighting this battle for more than five years. We at DHS central office who were tasked with preparing to move this latest integration forward knew that it was going to be an incredible battle of wills and the good people of SOS stood strong throwing up every roadblock they could think of to impede our forward progress. We heard every excuse on the planet from them from the minute we started asking questions.

They absolutely refused to provide us with information about their network and applications that were crucial to their organization; they played the movable meeting game over and over again; they defined new positions and moved people into them while stating that these people had responsibilities that were out of the scope of DHS central office. In other words, they pretty much, and in no uncertain terms, told us to fuck off in the only way they could which was to smile, agree, and then make damned sure that nothing happened. What should have happened at central office was that someone with some actual authority and maybe a testicle or two, should have gone out there with a very large stick and some serious attitude and told them that the convergence was going to happen, and that anyone who refused to cooperate would have their sorry asses kicked to the curb.

Of course, you couldn't do that in state government because someone would run to the union or the newspapers crying that you used bad language with them or some other bullshit excuse. This, of course, starts all of the other bullshit processes that I have previously outlined, and then you have yet another delay which is what they wanted in the first place. As I said, passive aggressiveness can delay projects for months if not years, and in this case it had been more than five years since someone had come up with a good idea, and much time and resources had been wasted achieving absolutely nothing.

The truth of the matter is that the technical knowledge to combining networks isn't really that rare, and DHS does indeed have the people with the technical expertise to accomplish such a task given adequate resources and time. Assuming an appropriate level of funding, and actual bodies to perform such a task, this project could have been completed in less than a year. But lacking the desire to do such a project meant that some SOS busy-body went around talking about combining networks, staff cutbacks and other things that were simply not true to instill full blown paranoia in the staff.

The mere mention of combining efforts at an agency like SOS can start an email avalanche the likes of which god has never seen. It is especially easy for technology people to dig in because they know something that you do not, which is to say that they know where all of the proverbial bodies are buried. Everyone in IT talks to everybody because at some point or another everybody needs something from IT.

You might notice that whenever anyone gets fired, it's IT that finds out about it first because HR needs him or her to lock whomever it is that they are firing out of the network.

On a side note, I loved the fact that on the fateful day that CZ terminated me that my phone was disabled when I got back to my office to clear out my desk. Just who the fuck did she think that I was going to call? If I wanted to call someone I would have used the one in my pocket and which they couldn't have touched if they wanted to.

During the course of this project, due to the fact that DHS is so unable to get its head out of its ass and,since one of the issues that SOS kept bringing up was that ITS didn't have qualified people to do the job, an RFP was sent out to get someone else to do it. The quotes came back somewhere around a million dollars for the project. Bacon boy developed an immediate sense of horror at the fact that these vendors wanted a million dollars to do such a simple task. I knew that he wouldn't bitch so much if his favorite vendor had been there, but they were too busy trying to get the Enterprise Email contract to bid on such a small job at DHS. BB immediately launched a campaign to convince everyone that this much money was ridiculous and that none of the vendors who responded were qualified to do it anyway and so the RFP was revamped and sent out again.

Meanwhile CZ began complaining that the costs to do this project had risen to an intolerable level and that she was only going to provide a few hundred thousand for the project. The opinion of all of the managers in ITS was that the project could be done internally, but due to the insistence of SOS that the central office was not qualified and the SOS desire to not step on any toes out at SOS, the project was sent out for bidding. By now BB's favorite vendor had been informed that they were not the top choice on the Enterprise Email project, and so since they were less busy, they decided to bid on the SOS Integration project. Do I even need to tell you which vendor got the contract?

Be aware that it was never the fact that the vendor in question is unqualified to do certain jobs at DHS, but more about how BB finds a way to circumvent the bidding process and steer all contracts to his preferred vendor, even when the whole technical team in ITS disagrees with his choices. Another example that proved this is that DHS had been trying to implement an online meeting system for the previous two years. Even though DHS already owns the licenses to the Microsoft solution for online meetings, BB has pushed his own agenda and gotten CZ to agree to a solution which is only provided by his preferred vendor.

By selecting a solution that has limited competition, you tend to eliminate the bidding process and are able to select the vendor of your choosing. When and if the solution is finally implemented, all of the agencies will of course want to jump on the bandwagon and the estimated total costs will probably exceed a million dollars in hardware, software, and licensing costs that could be used for something else important to the agency and the people of the state of Minnesota.

But to get back to the point, the bottom line of this is that the SOS integration project is five plus years in the making and little or no progress has been made for the reasons I have laid out for you and for many others too dull to explore. ITS employees have no real mandate to accomplish anything and no reason to stick their necks out for anyone else, no matter what they truly believe in. The system promotes failure and incompetence, and the unions protect them because it gives them strength in numbers, even when said employee is completely worthless.

The other failure in the system is that it should never be the responsibility of the staff to fight the battles required when major change is required or mandated. It should always be the responsibility of management alone to set the project and the priority of said project and to inform the respective agencies of these changes and mandates. It is difficult enough for an employee to walk into a hostile environment to perform an unpopular task without having to work without the support of management.

It is already difficult enough to work under a system that provides little direction, and it has been suggested by others that I file suit against the state for the year I spent working under incompetent management and the many false pretenses that were never part of the job description I received when asked to interview for the position. Although I am sure that I would probably be successful should I opt to go this route, and reasonably sure that the state would pay me to keep quiet, I also feel that this would allow the people of Minnesota to keep being ripped off if my problems with the system were to be silenced by my receiving a check that requires me to be quiet about the whole thing.

I also have issues with being the next black guy who files a suit claiming discrimination by a government entity. Yes, I believe that one of the major reasons that I was hired was because I am African American and because it would look a whole lot better it I fired EC than if CZ did it. I have also heard stories about state employees who happened to be African American running to the EOE office whenever they didn't get what they wanted. The EOE office investigates any and all of these accusations, and it protects these individuals because that is what they are paid to do, but I don't believe that should be the only and immediate fall back position for anyone who feels discriminated against unless there is some actual discrimination going on. Policies like that teach state managers that they should never hire minorities, or that if they do hire minorities and they turn out to be complete pieces of shit, you have to let them get away with it and this is no way to conduct business – no matter what the company.

Projects of an internal nature are important because they provide the infrastructure for the rest of the agency to conduct business, but deploying and managing these technology solutions does in fact take a village as it is said.

One month after I began at DHS, the conduit that holds the fiber connection that serves to connect DHS to its main service provider and to other state agencies filled with water and froze, killing most if not all connectivity between all of the agencies that relied on DHS services. Although the system was initially believed to be fully redundant, it quickly became apparent that the redundant links were flawed and that the circuits that were designed to supposedly fail over to alternate circuits simply failed to do so. We started receiving complaints about services going down and began investigating the solution immediately.

Because it quickly became apparent that we were losing fiber links to our main provider, we began the process of contacting them to try and get the problems resolved. The real truth was that the DHS redundancy circuits were never completed and it took a team of about twenty people to track down the issues. Over the next two days, the frozen fiber problem was located. OET, who was the provider of the circuits, began calling their vendor who maintained the circuits for them it too. It took several days to figure out exactly what was going on and where the failures had occurred. The engineers at DHS spent most of that time manually re-routing circuits and data from agency to agency, building to building in order to restore services and worrying about capacity issues

Almost everything in DHS ran over those circuits: the security system, video feeds, data backups, and pretty much every website that DHS provides to the general public, and although the engineers managed to re-route all of the critical services manually, much of the network remained down for several weeks. Several critical services that could have compromised the safety of everyone in the DHS building remained down, and DHS and OET spent a considerable amount of time pointing fingers at each other and making excuses to the customers as to why their services were running so slow.

OET was relying on the vendor to effect repairs as quickly as possible while trying to help the engineers at DHS route services through another circuit. OET also provided alternative fiber connectivity, which they had borrowed from another company on a temporary basis. I won't go into all of the details of what it takes to replace fiber in a circumstance like this except to say that if you imagine that you have a tube several hundred feet long filled with water and frozen you would need to use high pressure steam to thaw out the hose, pull out all of the offending fiber and replace it with new fiber. The issue was doubly compounded in this situation as the offending tube was hanging seventy-five feet above the I94 freeway and there was no way we could have closed off the freeway to effect repairs. You also need to understand that BB had originally been hired to design and implement the infrastructure for this redundant network and never bothered to complete it. Both BB and CZ made it absolutely clear that the only information that was to be given to customers was that our portion of the network had failed over as designed, which was a lie, and that OET had failed in responding in an appropriate manner, which was also a lie. Of course, she didn't want anyone to know that her highly paid Canadian consultant had allowed something like this to happen. Once the fiber had been repaired and services had been restored, much time was spent pointing fingers and providing jaded explanations as to why this happened and how to prevent it in the future.

The problem was not resolved before the next winter. Over the next few months, through the spring and summer of 2007, I continually beat on BB to work on getting the redundant infrastructure in and functioning before the snow flew once again. This never happened, and as of December 6th when I departed, the circuits were still not in. We had had many meetings, spent much time, energy and effort in trying to design the circuits, but this was another one of the situations where BB wanted to be in charge and held up the project by not providing information to OET as to what was needed or how it was to be implemented as was his edict from CZ. During the entirety of 2007, we withheld information from OET despite meetings that were designed to further our cooperative efforts.

And all because BB wanted to secure his position and CZ wanted to maintain her empire. A small part of me really hopes the circuit fails again over the winter so that maybe someone higher up the food chain will realize what is really going on at DHS.

In many ways, I have so much respect for the employees of DHS who work there and survive despite odds that are completely against them. I do understand that it is difficult to change such a complex system all in one go, but it would be nice to see that change begin to happen even if it is only a small bit at a time.

I began my position there ready to believe the rumors that I had heard over the years about government work, but still thinking and believing that it would be possible to do something positive even if the system was one with many flaws. I now know that a system is a thing that remains static unless some outside force exerts pressure on it to begin the process of change. I have learned and now know that the system is only flawed because of those who hold it dear to their hearts with no desire to see anything different.

Agencies, schools and other governmental entities suffer though endless bouts of bullshit from DHS management while trying to achieve the goals they were formed to provide, and the ones who end up losing are the people of Minnesota.

I hope that when this book is published, someone down there picks it up and reads it from cover to cover and then starts an investigation as to why things are the way they are. I don't care if they believe me, or the words that I have written here. They only need open their eyes in the general direction of DHS management, and the stink of inefficiency will roll off the walls right in front of them.

CHAPTER 5
SINCE YOU ASKED… MY CONCLUSIONS:

This chapter is the conclusion of this drama, but also includes a few suggestions that may serve to help should someone decide that the tales I have told in this book are at least worth investigating. There were many things that led up to me wanting to write this book and tell the tale of what was really going on there. There is simply no excuse for people to be allowed to corrupt governments to their own benefit, waste government resources, and continually rip off the taxpayers of Minnesota so that they might have a comfortable retirement with complete benefits. I began writing this book in my head within the first sixty days of starting work there because there were just so many things that really didn't make sense.

There was the time that CZ decided that we needed to have a meeting off site and that that meeting was to be held at her home for an entire day. CZ had often told us about her love of entertaining, how many people she could fit into her home, and how beautiful the lake behind her house was. Personally, who gives a shit? If this was indeed state business, then she should have scheduled the meeting at a time and place that was convenient for all of the people required. We all had to leave home early and drive 40 miles both ways to her home. Some people indicated that this would be impractical because they were allergic to cats, since we had all heard about three hundred stories about her cat. Her response to those people who indicated that they were uncomfortable with this arrangement was "so then don't come."

Here was a director who on her own insisted that we all come to a party at her home during work hours and refused to change the location of the meeting even though some of the people who were required would not be able to attend just because she enjoyed entertaining at her home. She cooked and invited us all to see the view of the lake, and yes we did discuss some work items. But we could have just as easily have done this in one of the very large conference rooms in the shiny new DHS building without driving eighty miles in rush hour traffic.

No one wanted to go to this, but no one dared say no due to her well-known tendency to bend anyone who said no to her over the fence. NT had sent out a message asking if anyone wanted to car pool and everyone declined. It wasn't that anyone objected to riding with NT, but that everyone wanted the ability to get the fuck out of Dodge at their own convenience and didn't want to be stuck there. CZ was quite visibly upset when we refused to stay after the meeting, but the truth of the matter is that no-one wanted to be there and we were eager to return home our families after a two hour commute detoured by the 35W bridge collapse.

There is the fact that CZ is off on Mondays, even though Monday is usually the day when all of the problems and issues that are come up over the weekend need to be managed. I understand the concept of telecommuting, but I do not understand how one telecommutes without a computer at home. All of us in engineering have spent many hours troubleshooting her blackberry because she is unable to use the thing correctly and for some reason or another "she keeps seeing dead people." What I mean by this is that she complains that people who have died over the years keep appearing on her device long after she had deleted them. This actually means that she either has not in reality deleted them or that she somehow synced with her desktop which still contains the information. Whatever the case, either she ought to learn how to effectively use the damned thing or give up all together and go back to using a pencil and paper and let the people of engineering and desktop get on with some real work.

The engineers at DHS are, for the most part, all good people, but have fallen in with the crowd that allows the system to be abused. The union guidelines very specifically spell out policies and guidelines as to what can and cannot be done to an employee and under what circumstances union representation can be utilized by an employee. This has the net effect of protecting the employee, but as I have already stated, it can also be used to prevent almost any kind of disciplinary actions be taken against an employee, especially when said employee has been there for a substantial period of time. Once an employee crosses a certain threshold in state employment, they have the unique ability to become fairly bulletproof. The net result of that particular loophole is that employees who are pretty much worthless can be around for years.

There was one instance when I asked an employee to do something, and that employee refused stating that they were busy. It didn't really matter that this was an employee who spent more time gossiping than doing any actual work, nor the fact that anything this employee happened to be working on was almost always supposedly compromised by the fact that someone else had not provided her the information she required to complete the task asked of her. Keep in mind that when I speak of these delays, I am not speaking of minutes or hours, but of days or weeks and that only constant badgering served to instill the sense of urgency you intended to this employee.

When I asked EC and this employee to come into my office to discuss this particular issue, she insisted on having union representation at the meeting. I agreed only because I wasn't doing anything of a disciplinary nature to this employee and I simply wanted to get it over with. During the course of this meeting, this employee informed me that she was afraid of me and felt that her job would be in jeopardy. She also informed me that she had overheard me tell someone the day before that they "were nothing" in the big scheme of things which was an outright lie as this is something that I would have never, ever said to an employee. She also threatened to resign, (which personally would have made me very happy), and the basis of her threatening to quit was that SB had done so. I found this quite interesting since she was one of the main people who had dedicated so much time to railroading SB out of there is the first place.

But you see, the problem here is that an individual can say almost anything and if they decide to lodge a complaint, the union has to investigate the issue no matter how untrue certain allegations may be. While this is understandable, what then happens is that the employee now has the upper hand because even something as benign as asking the employee to complete a task in a timely manner can be twisted into an incident where they may claim that you are harassing them.

Most employees who are bold enough to take this tack tend to realize this and then proceed in pushing the issue as far as they can. Employers who are already short on time are loathe to pursue the matter, and what they end up with is just another pain in the ass employee. This is one of the many reasons why CZ didn’t want to fire EC or SB. It would have taken too much time, and she had let the previous six or seven years expire without dealing with it, so her neck would have been on the chopping block. It was far easier for her to put mine on there instead. But here was the interesting part. That employee was going through a divorce during the first few months of my position there and having gone through one myself recently and knowing how difficult it can be, I was extra nice to her. I had cut that woman more slack than anyone else in the department. I joked with her, traded stories about the fact that we both shopped at Bath & Body Works, told her to sell the ring and buy herself something nice when she complained about money, and I generally tried to be nice to her because she was going though a difficult time in her personal life. And now you see what I got for my trouble? I should have taken my own advice and kept my eye out for the knife in my back.

After the meeting, I called EC back into the room and told him that he needed to inform the people of his team that the very next time I wanted to talk to someone as was my right as their manager, and they requested that a union representative be involved when there was no need, that I was going to get out the union book and use every fucking word in it to establish all of the policies and procedures for his department.

This meant that I would re-do all of the schedules for them to accommodate how I thought they should be instead of what was convenient for them. This meant that I would require two weeks notice for all absences and a doctor's note for all sick days. It meant that all four-day work weeks would be eliminated and that all projects would be scheduled and all engineers would be held to such a schedule and that disciplinary actions would be used if they were not. This meant that their cushy little existence of essentially being able to do as they pleased would come to a screaming halt faster than they could fill out an email to request a day off.

And I have to admit that I was quite upset at the way things were going on by then. These people didn't know what I was going through with my job or that the nut-job in the side office had asked me to essentially fire half of them and to beat the rest of them into compliant little pulps in whatever way I could manage.

It would not have been a good thing for me to walk in to my staff meeting and say to them that CZ considered most of them a waste of flesh and would be quite happy if most of them were to drop dead so she could replace them with a bunch of ugly fat little bacon boy clones who would be quite happy to keep their lips pressed firmly to her big fat ass.

In trying to not to waltz in and change too many things at once, and in trying to achieve the goals of the agency what I got were people who took offense that I actually asked them to do their fucking jobs at all. Even though I knew my days at DHS were numbered, I was beginning to get quite pissed off at the people I had been watching over and risking my jobs to protect them from the big scary one in the office.

I didn't understand how I was expected to implement policies and procedures when those same policies and procedures had failed to be implemented by people who had been there a hell of a lot longer than I had. I didn't understand why my director, who had asked me to implement those policies and procedures, would tell me that I needed to be careful not to step on anyone's toes while in the process of implementing them. Of course I was going to step on toes, as that is how you get things done with people who have no desire to change and who are not afraid of any repercussions when refusing to go along with the program.

It is never a fun thing to be firmly lodged between a rock and a hard place, especially when a tyrant, more interested in crushing the little people instead of discovering a way to remove the rock, controls the entire situation.

CZ's insistence that a contractor manage all major state projects and state employees (which I am sure is illegal) shows that her desire is that of maintaining control instead of providing those services. A contractor is not inclined to complete a job in a hurry, as that would affect their source of income. A contractor is more inclined to throw up as many roadblocks as possible in lieu of progress in order to extend their contract. Those roadblocks also tend to be of a nature that can more than likely only solved by said contractor, or that serve to extend a particular project.

In the case of AH, it would seem that his methodology is to expand the scope of projects as much as possible or complicate the design and implementation of these projects to a point where the details of any such project cause the original project to grow exponentially. At first I thought that his desire for so much detail was due to his desire to be thorough in gathering information. It quickly became apparent that his only desire was to continue his trek along a road apparently paved with virtually free money, and as I have said before, sometimes a project is simply what it originally started out to be.

One example I will provide is the LIST SERVER that a customer requested.

For those of you who do not know what this is, a list server is a server that allows one to send or receive messages to thousands of people or agencies with the click of a button. In June of 2007 an agency requested that we build a list server for them so that they could stop paying for the one that OET was providing them. List Servers are very easy to build and can typically be built without any software costs. I agreed to provide this server and since by this time I was already sick of the bullshit procrastination methods CZ nurtured, I went ahead and built the server before getting authorization. Once the server was built, I informed AH that I would turn the server over to the customer as soon as all of the signatures were gathered. Four months later, the customer had not received any info from AH and when I went to ask him about it he feigned ignorance and said that he would talk to the customer. When I left six months later, the final project charter had still not been completed. The List Server on my website, which is of equal capacity to the one that DHS required, was built by me in less than one hour.

Now you may ask me why I went around the system to get that done. I did so because it was easy to do, the customer needed it, and if we had gone through the system it would have never even been built. Not to mention that having been asked to rebuild some of the bad will inherent in the relationships with other agencies. It seemed to me that part of that process would be to actually provide some of the services that they were requesting. At least this way, the customer may eventually end up with it as it is just sitting there.

To provide you with an example of another one where we did go through the system, there is also the case where a customer asked us to create a very simple Sharepoint site for a project that they were working on. This site could have literally been created and turned over to the customer within an hour. But we decided to go through the process and we submitted the request to the Sharepoint team headed by MS. Remarkably enough, they approved this site for the customer.

We built the site and informed everyone that it was completed and the customer could use it. In less than twenty-four hours, we received an email from MS forbidding us from using the Enterprise Sharepoint site for this customer because they were not part of the pilot program and because they thought that we were going to build a separate site for this customer. Keep in mind that this was the high end, fully redundant, already paid for site, that was sitting there doing nothing because its funding had been cut and we were not going to be allowed to use it because the PMO office could not take credit for it.

Also, these are the same motherfuckers who are jumping up and down to manage all IT projects for DHS. If you think that the projects that I have already outlined for you are moving slowly, try handing over the rest of them to the PMO office and you will truly see things grind to a halt under the incompetent guidance of you know who and her crew. This all means is that Agencies no longer expect to receive these services from ITS for exactly the reasons I have outlined for you in the previous chapters, and it's quite a shame that it has come to this.

If the governor actually desires that these agencies move forward with his drive to excellence, he should take some of the money allocated to agencies for projects and instill an independent oversight manager for each agency. The individual person or persons tasked with the oversight of these agencies should be the final say in authorizing projects and the funding for each of these projects and quite possibly the agency priority for each of these projects. This would ensure that smaller agencies have some ability to have their projects worked on and in a reasonable period of time.

The person or persons tasked with the oversight of these agencies should also be an expert in the particular area or services that the agency provides. ITS would have oversight from an expert and certified technical project manager with considerable experience managing state projects and should also have reasonable knowledge of the laws and other criteria each agency is required to meet in order to successfully implement a project.

Projects for HCO and MinnesotaCare, and their funding, should have oversight from an independent healthcare professional. The oversight team should decide upon the viability of these projects and their priorities in the queue, which will prevent projects being allocated according to self-imposed self-preserving priorities.

All projects should go into the queue and a team of engineers and operations professionals should be tasked with implementing the smaller projects requiring little resources and funding. A good deal of the projects that were presented to ITS were small enough to have been completed in a matter of hours or days at the most. One example of these projects includes websites. A typical DHS standard server could in fact house many single but separate websites, and implementing a public website is about a fifteen minute process. Upon logging into the server to house the website, the administrator only need create a directory for the files that comprise the website, and copy the files into that directory. A DNS entry and an A record would then need to be created to point the website to that directory and then your website would be fully functional. Since most of these websites are completely informational, there would be nothing else that needed to be done. In the case of a website that houses actual data, you might add an additional hour or two to create the database and point the website at it.

If you have been visiting the website you will have seen my example of how to create a list server. I created that list server in about an hour. DHS is going on six months in creating theirs and to my knowledge, it still isn't up and running due to all of the political wrangling and bullshit that takes place in front of a project.

Sharepoint sites, which are currently all the craze at DHS, could be created in a matter of minutes. We created the infrastructure almost a year ago and creating a site that an agency would use to track documents and project status would take about 5 minutes. Yet agencies are not allowed to use this service without going through MS and are usually told to go to hell because the priorities of the PMO office is not to provide these services, but to garner favor with other agencies.

All budgeting expenditures with a value of more than $0.49 should be removed from the control of CZ and distributed by the oversight team to ensure that purchases marked for one project actually go to that project and are not incorporated into other projects. ITS has a habit of using this kind of control to get agencies to pay for internal IT projects as items that would serve to benefit ITS are simply tacked onto the projects for other agencies. If an agency requires a specific amount of storage for their project, ITS will request that the agency purchase devices well in excess of their requirements so that ITS can utilize that hardware for its own purposes. An example of this is that if an agency would require 1 TB of storage for their project, IT will purchase the single TB of storage to house the data which is appropriate, but the customer does not know that the cabinet ITS purchased to hold the 1 TB of drives has an actual capacity of twenty TB and that ITS will simply allocate the remaining 19 to its own purposes.

ITS should be completely restructured to represent an agency intended to work together instead of an agency separated into silos that only serve to separate and compete against each other for resources. If engineering, operations, application development and security would all work together as one team instead of four, projects would have a better chance of being completed because the onus would fall on the team instead of an individual manager to complete. CZ blames department heads for the failure of a particular task instead of the agency as a whole. Individual teams may have completed their portion of a project or may be waiting on another department to compete a task before they can continue to move a project forward.

That department may also have other priorities which were more than likely assigned to them by CZ and given instructions to complete that project at whatever cost, and so the newer project may be put on hold in order to meet her criteria. GO also has complete autonomy in scheduling resources and often sidetracks projects outside of his area to the benefit of his own projects and usually does so with CZ's complete authority. This only serves to create confusion and scheduling conflicts within the individual department and agencies as no one can ever be sure where their project falls in the list of priorities.

Contractors should be replaced with state employees or be hired for extremely limited periods of time when a state employee is not available or time restraints dictate that the cost of finding and training an employee would be greater than the expense of hiring the contractor. Contractors are an expense that simply eats into the available funds for projects and serve to create gaps in the knowledge of state employees by removing knowledge when the contractor is no longer working for the state.

All state jobs should be structured so that positions requiring certain levels of productivity are monitored and then renewed at the end of a certain period of time. If projects were assigned to employees whose productivity level played a distinct part in their reviews over a period of time, such an employee would be more inclined to be productive during that period. Certain types of employees or managers will imply that this methodology is untenable, however we as the general public should all be aware that this is the specific reason that our laws and election rules serve to allow for removal of someone who is not producing the desired or promised results.

Rules regarding information disbursement or other social services should be mandated by state law and not set at the local agency level. By allowing agencies to set their own rules and regulations you leave room for the fact that people not exactly inclined to provide certain services or information to the public can manipulate the system to the benefit of a select few instead of the public at large. When my director asked me to bury data that law insisted that I provide to the requesting news agency and falsify information requested by other agencies it was more or less the final nail in the coffin for my career at DHS, but in so many ways it was well worth it to be able to tell those requesting that I put my name on bullshit information to go straight to hell.

BH, who worked for DHS in the accounting department reporting directly to CZ and who also retired recently, was tasked with managing all of the internal and external billing for ITS. BH was in his mid sixties, and I am not exaggerating when I tell you that this grown man was absolutely terrified of CZ. This was because CZ pretty much went into devil mode complete with glowing eyes, spinning head, and spewing green vomit when presented with numbers or other information that she did not agree with or that she didn't want to escape the agency. She wasn't really concerned with the fact that ITS was wasting millions of dollars month after month, but was more concerned with the fact that someone outside of the agency might actually find out about it. It was absolutely amazing to see a grown man shake and shiver in fear whenever she spoke to him.

In the instance I described before, where I simply ignored her request until about an hour before the meeting on the Enterprise Email project, I met with BH to give him the final numbers to present to CZ. He visibly shook when he saw the number and in a cracking voice told me that CZ was really not going to like these numbers. I told him not to worry about it, but that I would take full responsibility for the numbers when she asked. He calmed down quite a bit and simply said, "thank you very much" and he even stopped shaking a little. I remember that day like it was yesterday, and I am still quite impressed that she instilled such fear in an adult man. I hated her guts, but fear was never an issue.

The problem with CZ is that she fell into the political groove of self-preservation without bothering to think about the reasons she was there in the first place. JB's management style is of similar intensity, but as far as I can tell usually well directed. If a problem occurred in a project that JB was managing, JB would simply call a meeting, figure out what the hell was going on, and then specifically define the roles of those she would task at resolving the issue, and thus issues were resolved. People walk out of meetings held by JB with a sense of purpose, but usually with their ass in tact for the most part.

A similar meeting with CZ is about thirty minutes of bitching and moaning, another fifteen or so defining exactly who the most appropriate person to take the blame would be, how to cover up the mistakes from the other agencies, and is usually completed with her putting her pen down like she had actually accomplished something and giving everyone the evil eye and a story or two about her wonderful life outside of DHS. All she had really accomplished during the course of this meeting was to piss everyone off and start them all wondering if there would be enough ice and snow on the ground so that on the drive home she might slide into a highway divider at a high rate of speed.

Overall, DHS could be a wonderful and productive place to work if not for the restraints its management puts on its employees. I challenge you all to walk down the hallway and look at the faces of everyone you walk by. Does the look on their face exemplify contentment and a sense of achievement, or does it convey a sense of frustration and disappointment? I'll give you ten to one odds that it's the latter of those two choices. I'll also give you the same odds that you often sit in frustration at meetings wondering why it's such a pain in the ass to get things done or even exactly what the purpose of that meeting is anyway.

My inevitable conclusion was that I could not work in a failed system and that at some point that I would write about all of the things I believed were failing in the system and how quite possibly they could be remedied. I decided that I was going to raise as much hell as possible, as loudly as possible, and to whomever would listen to me in an attempt to get the word out. I know that the management at DHS will have their own views on my motives, but since I did, on several occasions, attempt to talk to them about some of these things and I was shut out, I can only assume that they are part of the problem and not part of the solution.

Conversations with the DHS CIO were met with calm understanding and many excuses but little else. Statements made to Human Resources were simply ignored or met with additional false promises of investigating the faults in the system.

Conversations had with employees of DHS indicated an overall sense of frustration and disappointment as well as occasional anger, but as I have said, the state provides safe haven to those willing to embrace failure so why would anyone bother to say anything. These employees have also seen what happens to other employees who seem to not be entirely engaged in the failure of a system. So sticking one's neck out, even for something they strongly believe in, is an unpopular choice for those employees not completely committed.

The final thing that I wish to talk about is the employees of ITS and their respective managers or supervisors. As I have previously said, the engineers and architects in ITS are not completely responsible for their inability to complete tasks in a timely manner. The system is what has failed, and the employees have simply been pulled along in its wake.

EC needs to realize that the technology, management methodologies, and priorities change with time. The reason I was hired is the same reason that the next manager will be hired, and that is to effect these changes in an as efficient manner as possible. While it's unfortunate that CZ and GO decided that the only alternative to their inability to manage your hesitancy was through deception, they were right about one thing. That is that to manage effectively means having employees willing to adapt to those changes and the desire to work as a team throughout. It's a difficult thing to let go of one's empire having been the sole engineer of said empire since its inception.

One of the many things that he refused to realize throughout that year is one that many rulers failed to acknowledge throughout history. That is that inevitably such a tight grip on the status quo would only lead to rebellion and dissent. EC's employees do not respect him and spent many afternoons in my office complaining about his management style or lack of the same. The passive aggressive nature of the organization as a whole means that little will get done while smiles and nods in the affirmative are handed out like Halloween treats. It is effective in maintaining one's position, but not in gaining the respect of those who depend on you for services.

In the end what one has to ask them is how effective they were in spite of impossible odds and bad management, and finally how one feels about the time they spent trying to achieve something good under those circumstances. Change is difficult for most people, but should EC ever decide to embrace change and help DHS move forward, he may at some point end up sitting in the big chair that he so covets. It's not about holding on to the now, but about embracing the future. As DHS is more than likely going to be around for a while, albeit hopefully not in its current incarnation, there is plenty of room to grow, and provide the services it was formed to provide in the first place.

Addendums & Documentation:

Here is the job description that I was given when asked to interview and the reason I accepted the position. I was not allowed to do any of these things and all of these things were the responsibility of GO (the Canadian contractor).

STATE OF MINNESOTA

DEPARTMENT OF HUMAN SERVICES
Information Technology Services Division

3/30/06-rev.

POSITION DESCRIPTION

Incumbent:

Position: Information Systems Manager

Working title: Manager of Architecture and Engineering

Section: Architecture and Engineering

Prepared by: Chris Zehoski and Sandy Carlton

Manager's signature: Date:
March 2006

JOB SUMMARY:

The individual in this high level managerial position manages architecture and engineering staff with responsibility for design, development and technical standards for the Department. He/she has responsibility for the strategic use of DHS systems architects, engineers and security staff in relation to ITS responsibilities and goals of the agency. He/she provides long range vision, planning, and management for the design and continued development of agency technical infrastructure and the systems needed to support and connect the agency's network-reliant business applications.

This is a leadership role and **reports to the Information Technology Services Director**. The person in this position manages:

- Unit supervisors and high level technical staff;

- Design, development, and performance of a highly complex converged voice/data network;

- Design, development, and constant evolution of an enterprise-wide architecture, in alignment with a statewide architecture;

- Security Operations, including an Intrusion Detection system, to facilitate optimal use of appropriate technologies and data sharing, as well as network security critical to stakeholders, business partners, and the citizens of Minnesota;

- Agency-wide Research and Development projects; establishes agency technology standards, develops, endorses, and authorizes the release of products compatible with the technical environment and in compliance with statewide standards and directions.

- Procurement and investments in technology that may exceed $26 million annually.

SCOPE & IMPACT:

This individual will be expected to play an agency-wide leadership role in the planning and decisions related to the agency's information systems architecture and the technical direction the agency needs to take to meet strategic goals. He/she plays a highly visibility, agency-wide leadership role in the design, development, and alignment of the agency's architecture with statewide initiatives and the directives of the OET. He/she provides leadership to the management of major systems, in the development of integrated systems, and statewide standards for technology. He/she is a key contributor to the agency's IT Strategic Plan and the agency's legislative proposals that have IT components.

This position works in partnership with other members of the ITS management team, the larger IT community, including the Office of the CIO and major systems teams, and the Office of Enterprise Technologies (OET), and the agency's businesses.

ROLES & RESPONSBILITIES:

Manage critical ITS functions and services.

- Sets strategy for and manages core IT functions. Set and enforce the use of standards and best practices in relation to systems design, analysis, and management activities.

- Manage the creation, development, testing, and rollout of network-based IT solutions that are compatible with / can accommodate the composite systems operations of the agency.

- Employ the use of industry standards and best practices and enforce compliance with established processes and controls.

- Manage the continued development of the agency's enterprise-wide network's capacity to efficiently manage the grid of network-dependent major and smaller systems of the agency and business partners that interact with DHS via its systems.

- Manage the redesign and enhancement of the core backbone infrastructure that supports the enterprise's network and its interaction with the agency's major systems and applications.

- Manage the design and introduction of network enhancements/new components needed to sustain the system during periods of agency growth and the addition of new types of applications.

- Direct the development and enforcement of network security and access standards and protocols; Authorize and manage actions needed in relation to security breeches.

- Manage the network's contingency planning and the development of back up systems needed for continued services for critical operations and network recovery following major loss.

- Manage staff testing and/or evaluating network status, performance, and stability.

- Ensure the technical integrity of the network and its data, including the enforcement of uniform codes and standards for the agency's IT groups that use the enterprise-wide network as the access point for their applications and transactions.

A - 25% - A

Build and manage business partnerships and relationships.

- Manage relationships with statewide counterparts, the agency's major systems groups and business managers, and the breadth of small system/application users who rely on the network as the access point to its work, its data, and/or clientele.

- Manage a DHS relationship with the Office of Enterprise Technology and manage effective participation in the development of a statewide architecture.

- Establish and sponsor technical and business partnerships needed to:
  - integrate IT planning activities;
  - align related and co-sponsored projects managed by different DHS areas;
  - build the network's capacity and ensure its sustainability as environments change.

- Develop communications vehicles and partnerships needed to gain sponsor/stakeholder support of and input into network design, service, and performance changes and new directions.

- Represent ITS in budget and legislative discussions; direct staff providing systems specifications and justifying needed network expenditures.

- Manage section communications and develop managerial relationships with each of the major systems groups. Develop technical and business interfaces and joint processes with each area.

- Engage key parties in network planning and expansion discussions. Jointly steer long range strategic planning used to set the network's future course and prepare to meet future demands.

- Represent and manage staff representing the DHS network in agency /joint agency disaster recovery plans.

- Represent the requirements of ITS in major IT purchase discussions and the negotiation of network hardware, software, and service agreements.

<u>A - 20% - A</u>

<u>Manage agency R & D activities, projects, and use of project resources. Manage and account for the section's portfolio of projects.</u>

- Manage the section's portfolio of projects. Align and set project priorities with agency priorities; resolve resource conflicts.

- Ensure use of accepted project management standards, practices and protocols;

- Ensure that all projects have a stated business need that substantiates the use of resources and is appropriately sponsored by agency management.

- Estimate, revise and contain costs associated with the section's projects; develop procurement and sourcing strategies. Assess and weigh the tangible and intangible costs of projects vs. inaction, if not implemented.

- Manage staff conducting stakeholder analysis studies; oversee the section's project management relations and project communications with stakeholders. Ensure that project sponsors and stakeholders share a common understanding of each project's scope, products, and process.

- Authorize and manage the section's processes used for issues identification and resolution.

A - 10% - A

Serve as a member of the division's management team.

- Oversee division operations and new directions of the division in partnership with the ITS Management Team. Ensure that decisions and the needs of the section will be balanced with agency directives and overall needs of the division.

- As a member of the division's management team and larger ITS infrastructure, create a shared vision that incorporates current and future systems performance requirements.

- Integrate planning across the division and with other ITS groups; align and steer the development of the agency network, web-based, and data warehouse technology infrastructure.

- Build managerial partnerships with systems groups and business units across DHS that will enable the division to foster the development of cohesive integrated systems and the diverse systems performance needs of the agency. Recognize the needs of major systems groups as well as individual users.

- Provide long range leadership and engage the breadth of users at all levels who have stake in the IT design and service decisions of the agency.

- Develop technical and service strategies that integrate systems, data, voice & web technologies.

- Develop a cohesive customer service system that has joint management oversight and best utilizes the IT expertise and technical specializations of the division's staff.

- As a management team, research and develop the division's components of legislative and budget proposals. Align the section's legislative and financial planning activities and jointly plan for changes and new directions needed to comply with new legislation; identify structural, and cost, and implementation issues from an IT perspective.

- Develop proposals and implementation strategies that incorporate changing OET requirements and transition the agency's IT infrastructure and operations. Jointly propose and sponsor initiatives needed to meet the technical needs and service demands of the agency.

- Represent ITS on the Information Policy Workgroup. Develop and administer enterprise-wide policies and standards that protect the integrity and sustainability of the systems designed and supported by the division.

- Develop financial / resource management strategies needed to adjust to budget and funding source changes. Substantiate use of funds.

- Plan and oversee the incorporation and implementation of new technology and IT services initiatives into the DHS technology infrastructure.

- Represent the division, its management team, and its director in interactions with theOffice of the CIO and OET, as requested. Contribute to the agency's IT strategic plan.

<u>A - 20% - A</u>

<u>Manage the section's business operations and resources. Carry out the unit's personnel activity in accordance with applicable labor agreements</u>.

- Set objectives and performance standards for staff. Manage the development of its work plans. And progress reports. Develop and/or authorize the use of staffing strategies that facilitate critical project deadlines.

- Manage the section's budget and account for its use of IT and administrative funds.

- Evaluate the backgrounds of and hire qualified staff with needed IT, engineering, and network-specific credentials.
  - Acquire, develop the talent of, and engage systems architects, engineers, and security staff as members of IT systems teams, leads, and specialists.
  - Hire and/or ensure section access to needed business analysts and project managers.
  - Manage contracted vendors and staff.

- Perform all supervisory functions and account for the section's personnel activities. Ensure that all personnel actions are in compliance with the law, department policy and existing labor contracts. Evaluate staff performance. Reward, promote, and discipline employees, per the contract.

- Manage the section's reporting functions and use of data.
  - Oversee the development of new types of network/systems data analysis and reporting tools.
  - Develop data management and utilization partnerships with other sections of the division.

A 20% A

Workforce planning and management.

- Use IT and business relationships and IT service reporting and analysis tools to develop an IT workforce profile and package of IT services that aligns with the needs of end users.

- Assess the section's current workforce, status, and ability to support the technology of the future to evaluate the section's staffing and training needs and focus staff development.

- Anticipate the need to build competencies associated with new and emerging technologies.

- Translate the work of the section into needed staff qualifications and IT skills sets. Use trends data and other factors to analyze and project IT skills set deficiencies and gaps.

- Deal with mature workforce issues and prepare for attrition. Develop strategies for and engage staff in knowledge transfer activities, including the documentation of critical processes and jobs.

- Assess retention incentives to develop strategies for retaining qualified staff with needed skills sets.

A 5% A

RELATIONSHIPS:

This position reports to the Information Technology Services Division Director. In that capacity, he/she may be expected to act on behalf of and/or represent the director in division interactions and needed decisions. This position is an active member of the division's management team and may be asked to provide cross-over management coverage for other sections of the division at the Division Director's request. This position is a member of the broader statewide IT community and has ongoing interactions and project partnerships with IT management and personnel throughout major systems groups and multiple state agencies. He/she interacts with the agency's legislative, budget, and strategic planners, its policy groups, communications leads, contract attorneys, and security management teams. He/she is a member of the DHS management team at large, and in this role, associates with managers and supervisors throughout the agency.

He/she manages different units that are predominantly staffed by advanced level IT professionals having different areas of specialization. He/she has interaction and may engage in joint projects involving the Office of the CIO and OET. He/she becomes part of and manages staff assigned to matrix teams of people from diverse areas of the organization, and when needed, provide team leadership, as well as strategic and technical direction. He/she sponsors IT projects being managed inside and outside of ITS.

There is an external focus to this position that requires that he/she manage his/her relationships with political savvy and sensitivity to the conflicting and at times, competing interests and priorities of the section's clientele. He/she serves as his/her section's spokesperson in public interactions with external groups and individuals.

QUALIFICATIONS:

Core qualifications:

It is essential that this individual have demonstrated ability to manage resources and the technical infrastructure needed to manage the architecture for and maintain an enterprise-wide, high visibility, 24/7 accessed network infrastructure that has internal and external points of access. This position must have the resource management skills to be able to oversee both the business and technical sides of managing the system. He/she knows and is able to research applicable federal and state policies/requirements that apply when managing information systems in a government environment.

- Must have prior experience, the appropriate IT skills sets and capacity to strategically position IT resources and manage the technical operations of a major IT network with an adjunct R& D component.
- Must have experience and the demonstrated ability to plan, design and implement the disciplines of enterprise architecture, information systems architecture, systems engineering and security architecture.
- Needs an up-to-date understanding of information systems and technology and must know how it may be applied for business benefit.
- He/she must have sufficient breadth to his/her technical understanding to encompass all types of network interfacing technologies, e.g., web, wireless, and VOIP.
- Has the ability to provide leadership, vision, and give technical direction to teams of IT professionals.
- Able to review, evaluate, compare, and apply high level technical IT industry-specific detail.
- Able to develop and enforce policies and standards that apply to an IT environment.
- Able to analyze problems that have business and technical components.
- Able to quickly adapt to critical situations and operate while under emergency conditions.

<u>Advanced level human relations and negotiations skills with ability to:</u>

- manage relations with parties having conflicting priorities and agendas;
- negotiate formal agreements;
- manage relations with a diverse range of technically versed and non-technical stakeholders;
- facilitate processes needed to find common ground and help parties reach consensus;
- develop and manage interdisciplinary teams;
- apply strong interpersonal and communications skills, along with the ability to work in a collaborative environment, yet take a strong stand, when required;
- respectfully interact with and respect the diversity of his/her staff and clientele.

He/she must be sensitive to and respectful of the cultural and other differences that he/she will encounter in interacting with his/her staff, co-workers and when serving customers. He/she recognizes and respects the cultural, ethnic and other types of diversity of his/her clientele and interacts in ways that enables the members of diverse groups to understand his/her data and messages.

FREEDOM TO ACT:

He/she acts with wide latitude and under the supervision of the Division Director and is accountable to the agency's CIO. He/she acts independently with managerial discretion in relation to his/her section's systems activities, its business, and interactions with IT managerial counterparts. The position must be cognizant of and consider applicable state and federal laws and other constraints on his/her decision-making, policies, and use of resources. Significant policy, budget, and legislative issues and identified risks are brought to the Division Director for discussion and response. Problems will be addressed at the appropriate level.

Seems like a great job doesn't it? Too bad it isn't really the job they wanted someone to do.

Here is the email regarding The SCHIP data that was requested by Minnesota Public Radio. You will note the fact that everyone in the loop is only providing reasons that the data cannot be found as opposed to the best way to find this data. This is completely in alignment with edicts from CZ that other departments are to be given as little information as possible even when there are legal liabilities.

One of the main reasons for this is that by allowing the public to know that the network can be searched very easily, other departments and organizations will know that they were previously lied to when told that something was not available.

NOTE: For the sake of continuity the email is left in its original format, which means that you should read from the end of the email to the top in order to fully understand its context.

-----Original Message-----
From: Zehoski, Chris
Sent: Wednesday, November 07, 2007 10:18 PM
To: Watson, Vincent
Subject: Re: MPR Data Request (SCHIP)

Thanks for the clarification. Over time I have been asked repeatedly to confirm that **restoration is not possible**. Wondering with the new capabilities you describe, if this is a decision. In other words, do we have the ability to shut off the logging?

Chris Zehoski
Department of Human Services
Director, Information Technology Services
651/431-2149

----- Original Message -----
From: Watson, Vincent
To: Zehoski, Chris
Sent: Wed Nov 07 15:56:08 2007
Subject: RE: MPR Data Request (SCHIP)

Chris:

We keep email server backups for 30 days. We would be able to restore data for this time period only.

By labor intensive, I mean that we do incremental backups and then full weekly backups. This means that a full backup of the email servers will have to be restored and then each incremental backup will have to be applied in order for the 30 day period. I am guessing that this would take Larry or Steve more than a week to complete the restore and then do a search for the specifically requested data.

-Vincent

From: Zehoski, Chris
Sent: Tuesday, November 06, 2007 12:35 PM
To: Watson, Vincent
Subject: RE: MPR Data Request (SCHIP)

Vincent... This message contradicts the message that I sent earlier (which I sent only because I did not receive a timely response to the first inquiry) and does not specifically answer the question asked. What is the status of back-ups for the period defined?? Does email exist for Aug-Oct or only October?? What do you mean by very labor intensive? How many people over a few days time?

Chris Zehoski
Director, ITS Operations Division
651/431-2149
chris.zehoski@state.mn.us

From: Watson, Vincent
Sent: Tuesday, November 06, 2007 11:31 AM
To: Zehoski, Chris; Berg, Johanna M; 'Terhaar, Nina'; 'Smigielski, Karen'
Cc: 'Honan, David'
Subject: RE: MPR Data Request (SCHIP)

All:

Since we installed EMC in June, all emails in or out have been journaled so we should be able to search for emails since June given search criteria. Barring this effort finding anything or not, we can restore his entire mailbox for approx 30 days only. This can be done but will be VERY labor intensive and will take a few days at a minimum.

Please let me know what search criteria you would like us to search on.

-Vincent

From: Zehoski, Chris
Sent: Tuesday, November 06, 2007 11:14 AM
To: Berg, Johanna M; 'Terhaar, Nina'; 'Smigielski, Karen'
Cc: 'Honan, David'; Watson, Vincent
Subject: RE: MPR Data Request (SCHIP)

Vincent Watson will provide us with a status of back-ups for that period before the end of the day today. The email back-up system was designed for BCP purposes. ITS has the ability to restore email for a point in time, but does not have the ability to restore mail by person or subject. Search for relevant material in the Commissioner's mailbox would need to be done from his mailbox.

Chris Zehoski
Director, ITS Operations Division
651/431-2149
chris.zehoski@state.mn.us

From: Berg, Johanna M
Sent: Thursday, November 01, 2007 8:16 AM
To: 'Terhaar, Nina'; Smigielski, Karen
Cc: Honan, David; Zehoski, Chris
Subject: RE: MPR Data Request (SCHIP)

thanks Nina. Karen, I forwarded the request to Chris Zehoski last week - the email piece is in her bailiwick.

From: Terhaar, Nina [mailto:Nina.Terhaar@state.mn.us]
Sent: Wednesday, October 31, 2007 9:02 AM
To: Smigielski, Karen

Cc: Honan, David; Berg, Johanna M
Subject: RE: MPR Data Request (SCHIP)

As I pointed out in my original email to Dave, this information isn't part of the Data Warehouse, so I don't have any way to check on this. When I checked out who should be the contact, I was told that a discovery issue like this has to go through Johanna, and she was one of the contacts on Dave's original emails. I'll make sure she's included on this response, since she'd be in the best position to know how the original request was handled.

Thx.

Nina A. Terhaar

651/431-2144

651/918-0108 pager

Caution: This e-mail and attached documents, if any, may contain information that is protected by state or federal law. E-mail containing private or protected information should not be sent over a public (nonsecure) Internet unless it is encrypted pursuant to DHS standards. This e-mail should be forwarded only on a strictly need-to-know basis. If you are not the intended recipient, please: (1) notify the sender immediately, (2) do not forward the message, (3) do not print the message and (4) erase the message from your system.

-----Original Message-----
From: Smigielski, Karen
Sent: Tuesday, October 30, 2007 4:45 PM
To: Terhaar, Nina
Cc: Honan, David
Subject: RE: MPR Data Request (SCHIP)

Dave asked that I check in with you on progress of the back up issue. I'm out until Monday as is Dave, but would appreciate an update by then thanks.

From: Terhaar, Nina
Sent: Monday, October 22, 2007 5:30 PM
To: Honan, David

Cc: Smigielski, Karen
Subject: RE: MPR Data Request (SCHIP)

This information is not stored on the Data Warehouse and the Data Warehouse staff has not been involved in any SCHIP related analysis or discussion, so I won't have anything to forward to Karen. I will ck further into email and document backups outside of the Data Warehouse to see who can provide assistance in that area.

Thx.

Nina A. Terhaar

651/431-2144

651/918-0108 pager

Caution: This e-mail and attached documents, if any, may contain information that is protected by state or federal law. E-mail containing private or protected information should not be sent over a public (nonsecure) Internet unless it is encrypted pursuant to DHS standards. This e-mail should be forwarded only on a strictly need-to-know basis. If you are not the intended recipient, please: (1) notify the sender immediately, (2) do not forward the message, (3) do not print the message and (4) erase the message from your system.

HERE IS THE ORIGINAL EMAIL FROM THE LEGAL DEPARTMENT REQUESTING THE EMAIL DATA FOR THE SCHIP PROGRAM

-----Original Message-----
From: Honan, David
Sent: Monday, October 22, 2007 4:52 PM
To: Commissioner DHS; Wilkin, Tim; Colman, Loren; Kooistra, Wes; Osberg, Brian; Johnson, Chuck; Bronson, Christine; Berg, Ann; Berg, Johanna M; Terhaar, Nina
Cc: 'Singelmann, Lynne'; Barry, Anne; Rowley, David; Smigielski, Karen; Gunderson, Terry
Subject: MPR Data Request (SCHIP)

This communication is privileged (confidential) between attorney and client, and/or constitutes attorney work product, and is protected from disclosure outside of the attorney-client relationship by Minnesota Statutes § 13.393 and the Minnesota Attorney's Rules of Professional Responsibility. The information is intended only for the use of the intended recipients named above.

Hello everyone,

DHS has received a request from Minnesota Public Radio to inspect public information, if any, about the SCHIP that falls within the categories listed below. Karen Smigielski is coordinating DHS response to this request. Please assist in responding to this request by ensuring that the following procedures are followed:

1. Assign a coordinator for your business unit to identify and communicate with staff in your unit who may possess relevant data, and to gather any relevant data, if any, from those individuals.

2. Staff should review all potentially relevant data sources regardless of the form or format of the data (handwritten note, printed materials, emails or other electronic records, paper files, etc.)

3. The coordinator should review potentially relevant data gathered by staff in the unit and highlight (using a yellow highlighter pen or appropriate electronic means) any data that may be non-public or is otherwise problematic.

4. The coordinator should forward potentially relevant data to Karen on or before the end of business day Monday, Oct. 29 in the following manner:

· Email a PDF copy of the data that is responsive to this request (if there are more than 100 pages of data, please forward a detailed description of the data only to Karen by that date).

· In addition, if any of the data may be non-public, please indicate this in the email to Karen, and either electronically highlight or earmark such data in the PDF file, or forward the paper copy (with the non-public data highlighted as indicated above) to Karen via internal mail using mail code: C4168.

5. If you are aware of any other business unit or staff that may be in possession of relevant information, please forward this request to them, and "cc" Karen.

Requested Data

The categories of data requested by MPR are:

A. Handwritten or typed notes, including e-mail produced by certain DHS staff from Aug. 1 through Oct. 15. The request specifically includes Cal Ludeman, Tim Wilkin, Brian Osberg, Christine Bronson and any assistant commissioners and the Medicaid/federal relations staff.

B. Any versions of talking points, study plans, correspondence or other documents produced from August 1 through Oct. 7.

C. For talking points that are in an electronic form, information ("metadata") from document properties on when they were created, modified or accessed. To get this information open the document, click file, properties and general. Then click the top bar, move and OK. Open a new Word file, paste the info and print. If there are no drafts in electronic form, any information that is available about their creation.

D. Any notes or memoranda by Commissioner Ludeman or any other DHS staff member with representatives of the Governor's office on the topic of SCHIP between Aug. 1, 2007 and Oct. 7, 2007.

E. Any documents between the dates of August 1, 2007 and Oct. 7, 2007 in any department or commissioner's executive office subject files relating to SCHIP funding, including correspondence, printed-out emails and handwritten notes.

F. Any e-mails sent by or received by the commissioner relating to federal SCHIP funding that were preserved in computer backups of the agency between August 1, 2007 and October 7, 2007 (Nina and Johanna – I am hoping you can provide some guidance regarding this one.)

If send you have questions please, please let Karen Smigielski know. Thank you for your assistance and cooperation in processing this request.

David Honan
DHS Compliance Office

Caution: This e-mail and attached documents, if any, may contain information that is protected by state or federal law. E-mail containing private or protected information should not be sent over a public (non-secure) Internet unless it is encrypted pursuant to DHS standards. This e-mail should be forwarded only on a strictly need-to-know basis. If you are not the intended recipient, please: (1) notify the sender immediately; (2) do not forward the message; (3) do not print the message; and (4) erase the message from your system.

Remember what I said about CZ wanting to withhold our information and capabilities from other agencies. This is because if they knew what we were capable of, they might actually expect ITS to provide the services they are paid to provide. Here it is... straight from the horses mouth...

From: Zehoski, Chris
Sent: Thursday, November 08, 2007 7:02 PM
To: Watson, Vincent
Subject: RE: MPR Data Request (SCHIP)

Well...see what I mean? You said that you could do it and now it's expected. Wouldn't it be more efficient for someone to sit at Cal's desk and do that same search from his desktop as I suggested??

Chris Zehoski
Director, ITS Operations Division
651/431-2149
chris.zehoski@state.mn.us

From: Watson, Vincent
Sent: Thursday, November 08, 2007 2:18 PM
To: Zehoski, Chris
Subject: FW: MPR Data Request (SCHIP)

Chris,

I am being asked to search the following info?

-Vincent

From: Smigielski, Karen [mailto:Karen.Smigielski@state.mn.us]
Sent: Thursday, November 08, 2007 2:09 PM
To: Watson, Vincent
Cc: Honan, David
Subject: RE: MPR Data Request (SCHIP)

Vincent,
These are the back up e-mails we were asked to provide:

To and from Commissioner Cal Ludeman, from Aug. 1, 2007 to Oct 7, 2007
The search words would be “SCHIP” and “state children’s health care plan.”

Let me know if you have any questions. Thanks.

Email Messages & Other Documentation

- NOTE-

Some of the text of individual email messages have been deleted or edited where it may contain privileged information or other information that may serve only to compromise the security of DHS, its agencies, or peripheral networks.

These emails are included to document a statement in this book, however, where it would serve no purpose in including all of the specific technical information this information has been deleted.

Where passages have been edited or omitted, you will see the text:

"THIS SECTION OMITED BY AUTHOR'

This note is from a customer requesting information on the ability to do NET Meetings & screen sharing. Microsoft provides this capability in its server licensing for free, however GO wants to use a new solution which will of course be provided for by his preferred vendor.

CZ knows this, and you will note how she wants everyone to actually say that their request is unreasonable or otherwise undoable so she can forward this information as if it came from someone else. She also didn't know what the hell they were talking about anyway so she keeps asking for it to be re-phrased until she can understand it.

From: Owen, Greg
Sent: Monday, November 19, 2007 10:03 AM
To: Zehoski, Chris; Geiger, Barb; Watson, Vincent; Hoenigschmidt, John; Michelson, Laura
Subject: RE: Screen sharing software
It would be in conflict, and could be a replication of efforts,....so best we get engaged to understand what they are
proposing.
G
-----Original Message-----
From: Zehoski, Chris
Sent: Monday, November 19, 2007 10:01 AM
To: Geiger, Barb; Watson, Vincent; Hoenigschmidt, John; Michelson, Laura; Owen, Greg
Subject: Re: Screen sharing software

Sorry... Clearly I should have framed the question more carefully.
Would pursuit of a screen sharing solution be in conflict or be replication of other current efforts?? MeetingPlace
Manager or other??

Chris Zehoski
Department of Human Services
Director, Information Technology Services
651/431-2149

----- Original Message -----
From: Geiger, Barb
To: Watson, Vincent; Zehoski, Chris; Hoenigschmidt, John; Michelson, Laura; Owen, Greg
Sent: Mon Nov 19 09:36:27 2007
Subject: RE: Screen sharing software
I think the BRT should work with the business area to explore the request and develop a project charter to work towards meeting their needs. It is difficult to tell is the PMO has all the user requirements which would drive the solution.
Thanks!
Barb Geiger
Information Technology Services Division
ITS Operations Manager
651- 431-2117
barb.geiger@state.mn.us

From: Watson, Vincent
Sent: Monday, November 19, 2007 9:01 AM
To: Zehoski, Chris; Geiger, Barb; Hoenigschmidt, John; Michelson, Laura; Owen, Greg
Subject: RE: Screen sharing software

All:

Are they attempting screen sharing as part of a permanent solution for desktop meetings or is this simply for support issues? If this is for desktop meetings, I believe we have been attempting to implement a solution agency wide. I have no concerns about the ultimate solution, but would like to see it implemented as a whole solution if possible to prevent having to support multiple products.
-Vincent

From: Zehoski, Chris
Sent: Friday, November 16, 2007 5:21 PM
To: Geiger, Barb; Hoenigschmidt, John; Michelson, Laura; Owen, Greg; Watson, Vincent
Subject: FW: Screen sharing software
Please advise.

Chris Zehoski
Director, ITS Operations Division
651/431-2149
chris.zehoski@state.mn.us

From: Arvesen, Mary
Sent: Friday, November 16, 2007 4:46 PM
To: Zehoski, Chris; Caplin, Barry
Subject: Screen sharing software

Healthcare (MMIS helpdesk) approached Mary Swanson about using an Oracle product for screen sharing. They went to Mary because of the collaboration project. This is one of those situations where the business area came to us when they could've just done it without saying anything. What information do you need to give them any opinion, response, support or concern about moving ahead? Mary can follow up with them.

This is an email regarding how we may or may not implement a VOIP system as requested to other agencies. NOTE: CZ's comment about how slowly we might respond to their request. What she is really saying is that we are tired of these people and might get around to it eventually.

From: Owen, Greg

Sent: Wednesday, November 14, 2007 5:11 PM

To: Geiger, Barb; Watson, Vincent; Hoenigschmidt, John

Subject: FW: SOS Small Site VOIP Services

Attachments: VOIP Services Small Sites.doc

All,

fyi,.....Greg

-----Original Message-----
From: Owen, Greg [mailto:Greg.Owen@state.mn.us]
Sent: Friday, November 09, 2007 12:25 PM
To: Zehoski, Chris
Cc: Owen, Greg
Subject: RE: SOS Small Site VOIP Services

Hopefully this does the trick.

Greg
<<VOIP Services Small Sites.doc>>

> -----Original Message-----
> **From:** Zehoski, Chris
> **Sent:** Friday, November 09, 2007 10:53 AM
> **To:** Owen, Greg
> **Subject:** RE: SOS Small Site VOIP Services

Greg… This is great. Could we add something about lead time? We need something said to set the stage for managing expectations about how quickly (or slowly) we will respond to the types of requests and information we are currently receiving.

Chris Zehoski
Director, ITS Operations Division
651/431-2149
chris.zehoski@state.mn.us

From: Owen, Greg
Sent: Friday, November 09, 2007 8:37 AM
To: Zehoski, Chris
Cc: Owen, Greg
Subject: SOS Small Site VOIP Services

Chris,

Attached is a draft document outlining how we would provision VOIP services to smaller DHS sites and the criteria we would utilize in evaluating any request for such.

Let me know what changes you would like.

Greg

<< File: VOIP Services Small Sites.doc >>

This is a note from GO on how something got fucked up and we need to figure out whom to blame.

From: Owen, Greg
Sent: Tuesday, October 30, 2007 8:07 AM
To: Watson, Vincent; Geiger, Barb
Cc: Zehoski, Chris
Subject: Engineering Quality

Vincent,
Last week we had several incidents related to the VOIP system that caused, or could have caused end user service outages. Anecdotally, the root cause of these incidents seems to point back to poor engineering work,.....either not fully and comprehensively planned, or not properly implemented, or not properly tested upon completion.
The two most significant issues relate to the VOIP Witness system set up and as a result of improper configuration (on two separate projects), we missed two "threatening calls" from the public - not good.
So, I was hoping we could chat about some ways we may be able to institute practices across the organization that may help alleviate situations like this,.....you may have some ideas already in the works or being implemented, I don't know.
Two of the key items I would suggest would be:
- mandatory peer review and signoff of any configuration or engineering change to a "live" system
- implementing post project completion formal QA.
Maybe there are other factors relevant to this that can be considered as well. Can we have a discussion about this?

Greg

This is GO's way of telling me, "I own your ass, hurry and do what I want, and bring your people no matter what they are doing".

From: Owen, Greg
Sent: Tuesday, October 30, 2007 1:14 PM
To: Watson, Vincent
Cc: Geiger, Barb; Zehoski, Chris
Subject: CO Eng - SOS Integration Question Response

Vincent,
short notice, but we will need you and the project technical resource (Steve?) available to help with response to SOW questions we receive. Deadline for contractor question submission is today, with work on responses needing to take place tomorrow afternoon and Thursday morning.
Can you and Steve be available as needed?
Thanks,
Greg

This is a note about a project from GO, which essentially states "Take a whack at this, but don't let anyone see it until we can massage the info to our liking". GO was really good at following CZ's edict to not share data with other agencies.

From: Owen, Greg

Sent: Tuesday, October 30, 2007 2:13 PM

To: Watson, Vincent

Subject: FW: DHS07-023, DHS Network Domain Integration Questions from Caveo Technology

Attachments: 2007-10-30 DHS Net Intg Questions.pdf

Vincent,

please take a look at these questions,....we will need you and your teams input. Please don't forward this to anyone, or respond to anyone other than me on questions etc. related to this,....at least until tomorrow when we get some clarity with SOS and others on R&R's wrt this project.

Thanks,

Greg

-----Original Message-----
From: Swanson, Mary
Sent: Tuesday, October 30, 2007 11:31 AM
To: Lattu, Anna; Geiger, Barb; Owen, Greg
Cc: Garcia, Joyce
Subject: FW: DHS07-023, DHS Network Domain Integration Questions from Caveo Technology

Questions on the Integration SOW.

Greg -

Many of the questions are technical in nature. I don't think Anna and Barb have much availability this week, would you like me to schedule a meeting for us to o over the responses?

-----Original Message-----
From: Mark Sather [mailto:msather@caveoTechnology.com]
Sent: Tuesday, October 30, 2007 11:13 AM
To: Mary Swanson - DHS
Cc: George F. McNulty
Subject: DHS07-023, DHS Network Domain Integration Questions from Caveo Technology

Mary;

Thanks for the opportunity to submit a few qustions about the re-submitted RFP. We trust your clarificaitons will help us prepare our proposal.

If you need any clarifications about these questions, please feel free to contact me for additional information

Thanks,

Mark Sather, Senior Project Manager

Caveo Technology Inc.

Direct Phone – 952-922-8482

Cell Phone – 612-986-5074

e-mail – msather@caveotechnology.com

This is a note from GO which basically means… "I am being nice in letting you see this, but I will tall you later to tell you what to think"

From: Owen, Greg

Sent: Wednesday, October 31, 2007 11:00 AM

To: Watson, Vincent

Subject: FW: IMPORTANT - DHS Domain Integration Questions Responses

Attachments: Technical SOW Questions.doc

Vincent,

can you complete the CO questions on behalf of CO and send back to me? I will call you later to provide better clarity on how we are handling this.

G

-----Original Message-----
From: Owen, Greg [mailto:Greg.Owen@state.mn.us]
Sent: Wednesday, October 31, 2007 10:58 AM
To: Law, Mike; Martineau, Steven
Cc: Owen, Greg; Lattu, Anna; Beltt, Neil; Swanson, Mary
Subject: IMPORTANT - DHS Domain Integration Questions Responses

Mike, Steve,

further to a meeting we had today to review vendor questions received related to the Domain Integration SOW, there are several questions/responses that need your input.

Can you please review the attached document and populate with the correct answers or clarifications, as you see needed?

When done, can you send the document back out to the group above.

Also, it is important that we get your responses by end of day today.

If you have any questions, please contact me.

Thanks,

Greg
<<Technical SOW Questions.doc>>

On: I am in Canada right now and MN State Business will just have to wait.

From: Owen, Greg

Sent: Friday, November 02, 2007 3:52 PM

To: Beltt, Neil; Watson, Vincent

Subject: Re: BCP status updates to issues

Thanks Neil, I'm not in the office thios afternoon, maybe we can chat about next week.

Have a good weekend.

Greg

This message sent from my Blackberry Wireless Handheld.

----- Original Message -----

From: Beltt, Neil

To: Owen, Greg; Watson, Vincent

Sent: Fri Nov 02 15:30:25 2007

Subject: RE: BCP status updates to issues

Hi Greg,

No, I don't know where it comes from, but the stuff about cabling sounds like things I heard coming out of the HCO

people (Martin Daniels comes to mind)at the meeting I got stranded in a couple of weeks ago. I think this is generally

stuff from a status report that Marsha writes and maintains on BCP, but that's just a guess.

Neil

>-----Original Message-----

>From: Owen, Greg

>Sent: Friday, November 02, 2007 2:40 PM

>To: Beltt, Neil; Watson, Vincent

>Subject: Fw: BCP status updates to issues

>

>Any idea where this came from or who wrote? Let's not respond until we

>know where this comes from and where it is going.

>

>G

>

>This message sent from my Blackberry Wireless Handheld.

>

>----- Original Message -----

>From: Schwamberger, Marsha

>To: Owen, Greg; Watson, Vincent

>Sent: Fri Nov 02 14:14:23 2007

>Subject: BCP status updates to issues

>

>Hello.

>Would you like to update the status on either of these issues? Thank you.

>

>Description Open Date Status Person Assigned Notes/Resolution

>

Note:

"THIS SECTION OMITED BY AUTHOR

>Marsha Schwamberger

>Business Continuity Program Manager

>MN Dept of Human Services

>540 Cedar Street

>St. Paul, MN

>(651) 431-2151

Another note from GO, which really means… " I am just too damned busy to screw around with this. Make Vincent do it."

From: Owen, Greg

Sent: Tuesday, November 06, 2007 9:27 AM

To: 'Lapakko, Susan J'; Watson, Vincent

Cc: 'Beltt, Neil'; 'Owen, Greg'

Subject: Network Monitoring Status Report

Attachments: Monitoring-EnterpriseConsolidatedStatusOwen10-07.doc

Sue, Vincent,

attached is the October Network Monitoring project status report, which I updated. For next month, could you please assign further reporting on this to Vincent and place files in his folder?

Thanks,

Greg

PS, Vincent I will update RT with new dates, as I've put in this update.

Greg

J. Greg Owen, B.Sc., C.E.T., PMP
VOIP/Infrastructure Development Project Manager

Minnesota Dept. of Human Services
Office:651-431-2206 Mobile: 651-895-4018
greg.owen@state.mn.us

There is much more to this particular series of emails, but you get the idea.

www.ingramcontent.com/pod-product-compliance
Lightning Source LLC
Chambersburg PA
CBHW020200200326
41521CB00005BA/198
9780578009346